MAKIGUCHI ——————
THE VALUE CREATOR
—————————— Revolutionary Japanese Educator
—————————— and Founder of Soka Gakkai

by *Dayle M. Bethel*

New York · WEATHERHILL · *Tokyo*

First edition, 1973
Second printing, 1984

*Published by John Weatherhill, Inc., of New York and Tokyo, with edi-
torial offices at 7-6-13 Roppongi, Minato-ku, Tokyo 106, Japan. Protected
by copyright under the terms of the International Copyright Union; all rights
reserved. Printed and first published in Japan.*

Library of Congress Cataloging in Publication Data: Bethel, Dayle M
1923–/Makiguchi the value creator, revolutionary Japanese educator
and founder of Soka Gakkai./Bibliography: p.   /1. Makiguchi,
Tsunesaburō, 1871–1944. 2. Education—Philosophy. I. Title./
LB775.M3414B47 / 370.1′92′4 [B] / 72-92097 / ISBN 0-8348-0077-2

Contents

Illustrations (following page 64) ⸺⸺⸺⸺⸺

1. Tsunesaburo Makiguchi
2. Makiguchi and his wife, Kuma
3. Makiguchi with class at Shirogane Primary School
4. Organizational meeting of Soka Kyoiku Gakkai
5. Makiguchi and cadre
6. Josei Toda, second president of Soka Gakkai

Preface

This book tells the story of Tsunesaburo Makiguchi, a remarkable teacher and educator who lived in Japan during the years
that that country emerged as a modern nation and major world
power. It also tells part of the story of Soka Gakkai, the equally
remarkable religious organization that Makiguchi founded
during the later years of his life. Though well known as Soka
Gakkai's founder, as an educator Makiguchi is virtually unknown outside Japan. In fact, within Japan itself if one were

to ask the average citizen or even the average educator about Makiguchi, one would likely be greeted by a blank stare.

In official Japanese educational history Makiguchi is known as an elementary-school teacher and principal who invariably caused trouble in one way or another wherever assigned. He was unceremoniously released from active school work after twenty years of service in the Tokyo school system by being transferred to a school scheduled to be closed the following year. Yet, despite the anonymity and official stigma associated with him, Tsunesaburo Makiguchi is emerging today as one of the great educators of the twentieth century. The organization that he founded has experienced unprecedented growth since World War II and is today a major force in Japanese society. One cannot write about Makiguchi, then, without also writing about Soka Gakkai. Conversely, to write about Soka Gakkai is to write about Makiguchi because both the life of the man and the life of the movement are bound up together.

Makiguchi the Value Creator is the result of more than twenty years of research; many of those years were spent in Japan, working and studying. In 1969 a grant funded jointly by the Asian Studies Center, the Institute for International Studies in Education, and the Department of Anthropology of Michigan State University enabled me to spend two months in Japan engaged in intensive research on both Makiguchi's personal life and his work as an educator. During those two months, at times alone and at other times with a trusted assistant, I tramped the streets and alleys of Tokyo, where Makiguchi spent the major part of his productive years, searching for clues and leads that would help to fill in the still dim outlines of his life and career. These clues and leads spread in many directions, at times to remote villages in the Kanto plain, far from Tokyo. They led to schools where Makiguchi taught or served as principal, and where, in some cases, school records verified tenure and other facets of his relationship to the school.

They led to former students whose memories helped to sharpen the features of Makiguchi's personality, both as a man and as a teacher. They led to former teachers who had taught under his supervision and to colleagues who had taught with him. They led to associates who assisted Makiguchi in the 1930s in organizing the reform-oriented discussion groups from which Soka Gakkai traces its beginnings. They led finally to members of Makiguchi's family who, although reluctant at first, were most cooperative and gracious upon learning the nature of the research and the proposed uses of the information obtained.

In many respects this phase of research was the most enjoyable. For a brief period it was possible to be completely immersed in the life and personality of this remarkable man. At times it seemed almost as if that personality, whose form was taking shape through successive interviews and scanned records, was a present reality. Then, too, many of the people interviewed were elderly and in poor health. They would soon be passing on, taking their memories of Makiguchi with them. This realization added a sense of urgency and was a spur to leave no lead unchecked.

A word should be said here about problems of translation. Anyone who is familiar with Makiguchi's written work can bear testimony that communication through literary expression was not one of his gifts. His writing is extremely difficult to read, even for a Japanese, because of its disjointed and repetitive style. In one instance Makiguchi himself apologized for the limitations of his written work, indicating that it consisted largely of notes jotted down from time to time as thoughts and ideas came to him. Reading Makiguchi, therefore, becomes essentially a matter of searching for the treasures embedded in the volumes that came from his pen and attempting to relate these insights to each other in order to construct a framework or general outloook as close to that held by Makiguchi as can now be ascertained. In translating material from Makiguchi's writings, therefore, my concern has been to communicate as clearly as possible Makiguchi's salient thoughts and intent, rather than to slavishly imitate the original wording. Unless otherwise indicated, all translations from the Japanese are my own. It should be pointed out that Japanese names are rendered according to English style; thus names of individuals are written surname last rather than first, as in Japanese. Instead of "Sokagakkai," the form of the name used by the organization itself, the more usual journalistic form "Soka Gakkai" is used.

While I am indebted to a great many people for aiding me at various points in the research for this book, I would especially like to thank Mr. William P. Woodward, former director of the International Institute for the Study of Religions, Tokyo; Professors Carl H. Gross, Iwao Ishino, and Herbert C. Jackson of Michigan State University, East Lansing; Mr. Shukaku (Shuhei) Yajima of the Shoin Temple, Omiya, Japan; Mr. Tomiya Akiyama, Chief of Soka Gakkai's Foreign Relations Bureau, Tokyo; and Mr. Satoshi Ikeda and Mr. Kiyoaki Murata, both of Tokyo, upon whose works I have relied heavily for many of the facts concerning Makiguchi's life. Of course none of these people is responsible either for errors of fact that may remain or for the interpretation in this book.

In addition to the professional contributions of the people mentioned above, certain respondents provided invaluable assistance to the progress of my research. Among them were Mr. Kozaburo Nakabayashi of Tokyo, who generously donated his unpublished manuscript that recalls his impressions of Makiguchi as a teacher; Mr. Hirotaro Ito of Yokohama, who permitted me to borrow and make copies of priceless photographs covering his student life at a school where Makiguchi taught; Mr. Masatake Eto of Tokyo, who assisted with interviewing and spent many hours with me discussing and analyzing Makiguchi's writings; Mr. Tsutomu Watanabe of Chofu, Makiguchi's son-in-law and close associate in the development of Soka Kyoiku Gakkai, who graciously permitted me to have the only surviving copy of the ninth issue of *Kankyo* photographed for inclusion in this book; and Mrs. Sadako Kaneko of Tokyo, the widow of one of Makiguchi's sons, who besides contributing hours of her time permitted me to make copies of the post-card messages that she received from Makiguchi during his seventeen-month confinement in Sugamo Prison. And I am indebted perhaps most of all to my wife, Miyoko, whose encouragement and assistance have been invaluable throughout the research and in the preparation of the manuscript.

Grateful acknowledgments are also due the following individuals, publishers, and organizations for having granted permission to include copyrighted materials in this book:

American Anthropological Association, Washington, D.C., for "Revitalization Movements," by Anthony F. C. Wallace, reproduced by permission of the American Anthropological Association from *American Anthropologist,* Vol. 58, No. 2, 1956.

Noah S. Brannen, for "Soka Gakkai's Theory of Value," which appeared in *Contemporary Religions in Japan,* Vol. V, No. 2 (June, 1964).

E. J. Brill, Leiden, for "Trend and Problems of New Religions in Urban Society," by Fujio Ikado, from *The Sociology of Japanese Religion,* by Kiyomi Morioka and William H. Newell.

Harper & Row, Publishers, Incorporated, New York, for *Self-Renewal,* by John Gardner.

Japan Quarterly, Tokyo, for "Soka Gakkai and Komeito: The Advance of a New Religion into Politics," by Kazuo Kasahara, which appeared in Vol. XIV, No. 3, July–September, 1967.

Little, Brown and Company, Publishers, Boston, for *The Right to Create,* by Judith Groch.

The Macmillan Company, New York, for *The Rush Hour of*

the Gods, by H. Neill McFarland. Copyright © 1967 by H. Neill McFarland.

Charles E. Merrill Publishing Company, Columbus, Ohio, for *Intellectual Foundations of Modern Education,* by William E. Drake. Published by Charles E. Merrill Books, Inc.

Oxford University Press, New York, for *The Sociological Imagination,* by C. Wright Mills.

Random House, Inc., New York, for *Beyond the Ruling Class,* by Suzanne Keller. Copyright © 1963 by Random House, Inc.

Seikyo Press, Tokyo, for the *Complete Works of Daisaku Ikeda,* Vol. I; for "Great Cultural Movement: From Mechanistic to Humanistic Society" and "Youth Let's Advance Toward a New Day," by Daisaku Ikeda; and for *The Philosophy of Value,* by Tsunesaburo Makiguchi.

University of Michigan School of Education, Ann Arbor, for *John Dewey in Japanese Educational Thought,* by Victor Kobayashi.

University of Pennsylvania Press, Philadelphia, for two figures from *Anthropology and Education,* edited by Frederick C. Gruber; and for "Schools in Revolutionary and Conservative Societies," by Anthony F. C. Wallace, from *Anthropology and Education.*

University of Texas, Department of Cultural Foundations of Education, Austin, for the review of *Crisis in the Classroom: The Remaking of American Education,* by Van Cleve Morris, which appeared in *Educational Studies,* II, Nos. 1 and 2, Spring–Summer, 1971.

University of Washington Press, Seattle, for *Sōka Gakkai, Builders of the Third Civilization,* by James Allen Dator. Copyright © 1969 by the University of Washington Press.

Makiguchi the Value Creator

Introduction ——————————————————————————

The study of the development and growth of a pedagogy capable of promoting the self-actualization of learners is fascinating and exciting. Invariably one finds as one examines the historical record that the search for a humane pedagogy has gone hand in hand with a struggle to free education and educators from the bonds of traditional pedagogical concepts and methods. This struggle has taken many forms, but in most instances it involves a clash between two diametrically opposed models of the

17

learning process, one a dialectical, or traditional, model, the other a dialogical, or open, model.*

In the traditional, or dialectical, model the learner is perceived as empty, a passive recipient who must be filled up by one who has been previously filled and who is in possession of of knowledge. The key element in this model is authority. However, in the open, or dialogical, model the learner is perceived as a dynamic organism interacting with his environment and being changed in significant ways by that interaction. The teacher who chooses this model within which to carry on the educating process perceives himself not as an authoritative "knower" who transmits knowledge to the mind of the learner but rather as a guide or facilitator who assists the learner in gaining maximum benefit from his interaction with his environment. The key element in this model is interaction itself, or encounter.

Scholars and educators of the English-speaking world have available to them many volumes that deal with this search for a humane pedagogy within the western-European cultural tradition. However, very little is available in English concerning this search in non-Western cultures. In view of this, the study of the life and thought of such educators as Tsunesaburo Makiguchi can be revealing and rewarding. Makiguchi immersed himself in this search, within his own culture, for more than half a century. Out of his battles with Japanese educational structures of his time and his association with a few like-minded colleagues there emerged pedagogical views and ideas that are worthy of study by English-speaking scholars, worthy in their own right and also because these views and ideas seem likely

---

*The use of this particular terminology in describing these two models has been suggested by William E. Drake. See his *Intellectual Foundations of Modern Education* (Columbus, Ohio: Charles E. Merrill Books, Inc., 1967), pp. 341–42.

to have significant impact on Japanese society during the years ahead.

The acceleration of Japan's economic development following the Meiji Restoration in 1868 led to a situation in which Japan and the United States entered the twentieth century in roughly comparable states in terms of the accumulation of technological knowledge and industrial development.* Thus, although the cultures of the two countries were vastly different, they began the century facing common problems, needs, and concerns. In the United States, during the late nineteenth century and the first half of the twentieth, John Dewey was a pivotal figure in the response of American culture in general and American education in particular to the needs of people as human beings in a technological society. In Japan, if allowance is made for a time lag in the acceptance of Makiguchi's views by Japanese society, it may be said that Makiguchi played a similar role. As will be noted later in more detail, the quality and merits of Makiguchi's educational thought and proposals were largely overlooked and rejected by the Japanese during his lifetime and are just now coming to be recognized by some members of Japanese society.

Makiguchi and Dewey were contemporaries, Dewey having been born in 1859 and Makiguchi in 1871. Not only did they face common problems in their respective countries, but they shared a common intellectual heritage. Both were inspired and challenged by the great educational reformers of Europe: Comenius, Rousseau, Pestalozzi, Herbart, and others; both were deeply influenced by early pioneers in the field of sociol-

---

*For a discussion of Japan's "forced march to industrialization," which resulted, within a generation of the revolution of 1868, in the transition of Japan from an almost purely agrarian to a predominantly industrial economy, see Thomas C. Smith, *Political Change and Industrial Development in Japan: Government Enterprise, 1868–1880* (Stanford, Cal.: Stanford University Press, 1955).

ogy; finally, both Makiguchi and Dewey had to come to grips, as did their contemporaries, with the great nineteenth-century intellectual issues having to do with the nature of science and evolution and their import for human life.

This common intellectual heritage was a vital factor in the development and growth of both men. At the same time, both recognized early in their educational careers that the new needs and new demands of people in a technological age made necessary the plowing of new ground, the creating of new structures, and the reforming of old structures. Beyond this, they saw—as others have seen more recently—that as "our technological, scientific, and urbanized civilization moves forward with ever-increasing tempo, there must, of necessity, be some underlying principle of order, some scheme of values, some sense of purpose that extends beyond the material order of things."[1] Makiguchi and Dewey must be understood in terms of this search for an underlying order, for common human values, for meaning and purpose. In their respective cultures this search led them to formulate pragmatic conceptions of man and the world embodying the revolutionary implications of science and evolution.

It is widely recognized that in the United States pragmatism represents an indigenous philosophical development. American pragmatism reflects the social, economic, and political dimensions of American life of the century roughly from 1850 to 1950, during which it was born and grew to maturity. But while pragmatism was an indigenous development in America, it was not new in the sense that it had no connections with the wider movement of human thought.* On the contrary, as

---

*For two excellent works dealing with the development of pragmatism in America with particular reference to education, see John L. Childs, *Education and the Philosophy of Experimentalism* (New York: The Century Company, 1931) and C. Wright Mills, *Sociology and Pragmatism: The Higher Learning in America* (New York: Paine-Whitman Publishers, 1964).

Charles Peirce, William James, and other early scholars of the pragmatic school in America freely admitted, there were important continuities between their thought and that of earlier European philosophers, particularly Kant, John Stuart Mill, and Darwin.

It will be almost an afterthought to point out that John Dewey stands today as American pragmatism's chief spokesman. Without Dewey, as John Childs points out, it is doubtful that the ideas of Peirce and James would have developed into an indigenous American philosophic movement.[2] It was also Dewey who initially grasped the significance that the new philosophy bore for education. In the same way, Makiguchi represents and speaks for an indigenous philosophic movement in Japan. That the Japanese for the most part failed to recognize the significance of Makiguchi's work and thought in no way diminishes his stature as an educator and philosopher. On the contrary, the neglect and rejection of Makiguchi accentuates today the significance of his work and his contribution to contemporary educational thought.

The educational philosophy and pedagogy that grew out of Makiguchi's struggle to integrate the diverse philosophies in his cultural heritage and to relate them to practical educational needs represents an important contribution to the history and philosophy of education in Japan. In addition to this, as the founder of Soka Gakkai, Makiguchi contributed to the growth and development of one of the unique social phenomena of the contemporary international scene. The growth of this movement from approximately three thousand followers before World War II to well over ten million today is now well documented. Included in this number is a significant overseas membership, which according to the California headquarters of Soka Gakkai's American affiliate, Nichiren Shoshu of America, numbers more than 200,000 members in North America alone. As a lay organization of the Nichiren Shoshu sect of

Buddhism, Soka Gakkai's professed aim is the realization of a society that combines the happiness of the individual with the prosperity of all society. Komeito, the political party that Soka Gakkai organized and nurtured until it became a separate organization in 1970, has become one of the more powerful parties in Japanese politics. The religious, financial, human, and political resources that Soka Gakkai commands in contemporary Japan make it of key importance both in that country and in the international community.

Makiguchi's educational philosophy and pedagogy are integral elements of the educational and ideological foundations of Soka Gakkai, which alone makes their study valuable to Western scholars. But worthy of note too is the possibility that Soka Gakkai, in its present efforts to implement Makiguchi's proposals, may be pointing some new directions in the ordering of educational priorities. This is examined in chapter five.

A central concern throughout this book is the role of education and the educator in social and cultural change. As a result of this general interest and concern for the relationship between education and change, I brought the following questions to the book: To what extent can a reform-minded member of a social system bring about change in that system? Under what conditions and by what means can such change be effected? How important is education in effecting intentional and directed change? What kinds of priorities in the matters of learning contribute to meaningful and positive change? Is there a relationship between the value structure of a social and cultural system and change within the system? How can the dignity and worth of individuals be respected in societies in which change is occurring? Such questions pointed to the need for a general theoretical framework within which data could be analyzed and interpreted. After considering several possible theoretical models I chose for this purpose a theory of social and cultural change that has grown out of the work of the educational anthropologist Anthony F. C. Wallace.

Wallace's model is considered in chapter five. It may be good at this point, however, to outline the general elements of the model. The primary concept is the "revitalization movement." A revitalization movement, as defined by Wallace, is "a deliberate, organized, conscious effort by the members of a society to construct a more satisfying culture."[3] Any given society may be studied or analyzed in terms of the relationship of a revitalization movement or movements to it.[4] Thus in Wallace's terms a revolutionary society is one in which a revitalization movement is developing. A society in which a revitalization movement has succeeded in achieving its objectives and establishing its values as the predominant values of the society is defined as a conservative society. Finally, a society that mobilizes its resources to stamp out an emerging revitalization movement and to maintain the values of the existing order is defined by Wallace as a reactionary society.

Wallace admits that in reality no society could be wholly one or the other of these three types. He suggests, however, that it seems reasonable to consider one value orientation or another predominant in a given group, such as the political, economic, or religious leadership of a society, during a stated period. Likewise, this tripartite classification may be used to characterize different time periods in the same society. Wallace believes that we may expect these orientations to change in a definite order. Thus, "a society which is now revolutionary will, if it changes, become conservative, next reactionary, and again most probably revolutionary."[5] Over centuries and millennia any given society "is apt to follow a roughly cyclical path through revolution, conservatism, and reaction, over and over again."[6] At this point the provisions for formal education in a society become of strategic importance. The reason for this, according to Wallace, is that associated with each of the predominant value orientations is a philosophy of schooling that characteristically assigns priorities in regard to the things taught in schools.

In summary, then, the historical data obtained through interviews and through study of primary and secondary sources is handled here in two ways. Emphasis is placed, first of all, on the recording, analyzing, and evaluating of the data on Makiguchi toward the end of formulating an objective and realistic assessment of the man, his educational thought, and the movement to which he gave birth. Secondly, the theory of social and cultural change outlined above is employed as a means to interpret and evaluate the implications of Makiguchi's educational thought and practice within the larger context of societal reform and reform movements in general.

1 Family Life and Environmental Influences ————

———————————————————— *Personal Life and Education*

Tsunesaburo Makiguchi was born on June 6, 1871, the third year of the Meiji era (1868–1912), in Arahama-mura, Niigata Prefecture, a small village in northwestern Japan. Only a few isolated facts are known about his early life: he was the first son of Chomatsu Watanabe; his mother's name was Ine; and

25

his parents named him Chohichi. When Makiguchi was still very young, his father abandoned him and his mother. At the age of three the boy was left with the family of Zendayu Makiguchi, an uncle. We know that the mother met her son secretly from time to time until she attempted traditional murder-suicide by jumping into the Japan Sea with Makiguchi in her arms. They were rescued but the boy never saw his mother after that.[1]

Rough and mountainous land with sandy, unproductive soil surrounds Arahama. Eking out a living in this area, whether from the sea or from the soil, is hard. The word "Arahama" itself, which means desolate beach, suggests something of the bleak and poverty-stricken character of the community. At the time of Makiguchi's birth the life of commoners in this area was particularly difficult.

Something of the tenor of life of this period can be seen in an incident that occurred in the year of Makiguchi's birth. The leaders of the new revolutionary government of Japan were particularly anxious to increase agricultural production in order to undergird their plans for national development. They exerted severe pressure upon farmers to increase yields. The response of farmers in the Arahama area was a rebellion protesting the excessive work demanded by the authorities, which resulted in the execution of seven farmers.[2] The people of this area also perceived as threats two other policies of the new government. One was universal military conscription; the other, six years of compulsory elementary education. Both policies interfered with farm labor practices and needs.

Such was the situation surrounding Makiguchi's birth and early years. When he was in the fourth grade, his studies and a general emigration of local people to Hokkaido gave birth in his mind to an ambition to see this frontier area. The ambition grew until, sometime in his fourteenth or fifteenth year, he left Zendayu Makiguchi's family and set out by himself for

Hokkaido, where he lived for a time with an uncle, Shiroji Watanabe, in the city of Otaru. Because the Watanabe family was too poor to send Makiguchi to high school, he obtained a job with the Otaru police department as an errand boy. He also studied to pass a government examination that would qualify him to take college entrance examinations. This studiousness and the dependability exhibited on his job so impressed the chief of police that when he moved to Sapporo he invited Makiguchi to go along with him and enroll in Sapporo Normal School. Makiguchi accepted the invitation.

In 1891, two years after moving to Sapporo, he entered the normal school as a third-year student. Until he was twenty-two he used the name given to him by his parents, but he changed his name to Tsunesaburo Makiguchi in 1893, just before he graduated. Something of Makiguchi's interest in and affinity for the field of education must have been apparent in his work at the normal school, for upon graduation he was offered a position as a supervising teacher in the primary school attached to the normal school, a position that he accepted and held for eight years.

In 1894, a year after joining the normal school staff, Makiguchi married Kuma, the second daughter of Kumataro Makiguchi. To this union eight children were born, four boys and four girls. Tragedy in the form of the sickness and death of his children struck repeatedly during the last twenty years of Makiguchi's life. Four of his children died during the eight-year period from 1924 to 1932. His second son died in 1924 at the age of twenty-three; the fourth son died in 1928 at the age of nineteen; the first son died in 1929 at the age of thirty-one; the fourth daughter died in 1932 at the age of fourteen. Twelve years later, while he was consigned to solitary confinement in Sugamo Prison for refusing to cooperate in certain religious ceremonies and practices then required by the Japanese government, Makiguchi received word that his remaining son had been killed in battle in World War II. Shortly after receiving this news and while still in prison, Makiguchi died, on November 18, 1944. He was seventy-three.

─────────────── *Political and Intellectual Environment*

Born during the first uncertain years of the Meiji era, Maki-guchi's childhood and youth spanned both the initial intense debate among Japanese leaders and intellectuals as to the direction the new Japan should take and the resolution of that debate in favor of the traditionalists and the Confucianists. By the time Makiguchi began his teaching career in 1893 the die was cast. The direction of Japanese educational thought had been determined during the 1880s, the legal expression of which was contained in the Constitution of 1889 and the Imperial Rescript on Education of 1890.*

Robert Epp effectively described the implications of this debate and its outcome for Japanese education and society when he observed that basically at issue was the question of whether the aim of education in the new Japan should be that of building subjects or of building citizens.[3] Some Japanese insisted that a strong Japan could be built, finally, only by citizens, only by people educated to be independent and self-assured.

Those who favored this course hoped that people thus educated would be so little the servile subject that they would not

*For further information on this period of change, see Shimosa Idditti, *The Life of Marquis Shigenobu Okuma: A Maker of New Japan* (Tokyo: Hokuseido Press, 1940), pp. 209–19. See also Nobutaka Ike, *The Beginnings of Political Democracy in Japan* (Baltimore: Johns Hopkins University Press, 1950), p. 188 and Edwin O. Reischauer et al., *East Asia: The Modern Transformation* (Boston: Houghton Mifflin, 1965), pp. 286–88.

hesitate to defend their freedom, even if the entire government should be against them. Others, however, believed that only obedient and loyal men could construct the new Japan. Education, therefore, should have as its aim the building of loyal subjects. The latter group won the debate. Consequently, the new Japan "was to be built by subjects, not citizens. It would be built under careful direction from above. . . . The best builder was a man trained to be loyal and obedient, not free and equal."[4] This general direction of Japanese educational thought was maintained with periodic reinforcement through the end of the Pacific War.

Makiguchi's life and educational career must be seen and evaluated against the background of this debate and its outcome. Nowhere in his writings is there direct reference to the debate or to the contrasting educational philosophies encompassed by it. He did not question directly the policies of the government or the ends toward which education was used by the government. Rather, his criticisms were leveled at Japanese teachers and educators for their tendency to be bound by traditional ideas and practices or to accept without analysis and understanding whatever educational ideas happened to be popular in a given period.

At the same time Makiguchi's entire educational career was a protest against the production of subjects. While he managed to keep from bringing the wrath of the national government down upon him, the educational philosophy that he preached and the educational practices he advocated during the decades prior to World War II clearly conflicted with the overall educational policies of the government. It was not his revolutionary educational ideas, however, but religious convictions acquired late in life that led to his imprisonment during World War II. Makiguchi's efforts to bring about reform in Japanese education, his failure, and his turn to religion for the power to accomplish the desires and objectives that haunted and drove him for half a century create a story that is both fascinating and inspiring and one that affords significant insights for contemporary educators.

2 Professional Life

Sapporo Normal School

While information about his years of teaching in Sapporo is limited, the scattered bits and pieces that have come to light are important for glimpses they give of Makiguchi as a person and also for background against which later developments can be seen and understood. One source indicates, for example, that because he was always easy to approach with questions and problems Makiguchi was extremely popular with the student teachers he supervised.[1] It is also clear that he early became highly critical of the educational practices of his day as they affected the lives of children. His criticisms of Japanese education will be discussed later. Here suffice it to note that in Makiguchi's view Japanese education was stifling and destroying the creative potential of children rather than releasing and developing that potential. One can detect in his writings of this period a sense of mission and personal responsibility in calling into question the educational practices of his day. Satoshi Ikeda, in his biography of Makiguchi, suggests that the idea of the individual as a creator of value began to emerge here also.[2]

Early in his teaching experience, Makiguchi began to conceive the idea of attacking the problems of education through the study of geography. His fascination with this field of study can be traced to at least three sources. First of all, after the centuries of seclusion of the Tokugawa period (1603–1868) there was among Japanese a general interest in foreign lands. In a very real sense the study of geography opened up new worlds to Japanese students. Makiguchi undoubtedly shared this general enthusiasm for geography. Beyond this he was deeply influenced by two books, one of which was Kanzo Uchimura's *Chijinron* (Theory of Land and People), published in 1894; the other was *Nihon Fukeiron* (Theory of Japanese Landscape), by Shigetaka Shiga.

Geography, to Makiguchi, was much more than a study of land areas, climate, natural resources, and so forth. Although what he meant by geography included the study of these things, his primary focus was on the people who live within geographic areas, the relation of people to land and land to people. Furthermore, although Makiguchi was interested in geography as a subject of study in itself, his efforts were directed primarily to the use of geographic studies in the education of children. He believed, at this period in his life, that geography could be used as a central, unifying point around which the entire elementary school curriculum could be organized. In this way, he felt, the many weaknesses of education as it then existed could be overcome.

These convictions led him to the idea of writing a geography book for use by elementary school teachers. Accordingly, every spare moment during a period of nearly ten years was spent in collecting material and working on this project. According to students who were taught by him, Makiguchi *sensei* (teacher) always had a piece of paper or a used envelope tucked in his kimono on which he jotted down ideas whenever they happened to come to him.[3] Summers, between terms of teaching, frequently found him making the arduous trip to Tokyo to search for books and to come in contact with scholars and educators from whom he could get new ideas and with whom he could test his own.

There were likely many times during these years in Hokkaido when Makiguchi longed to be located permanently in Tokyo. There he would be at the cultural heart of the country. He would be able to keep in touch with other scholars, have access to libraries and bookstores, and be in a position to find a publisher for the book he dreamed of writing. The opportunity to make the move came in 1901. But it came about as a result of an unfortunate situation for which Makiguchi was held responsible.

In order to understand the turn of events at this time one must know something of the life of students at Sapporo Normal School. The general nature and atmosphere of student life as it then existed can be described in two words: rigid discipline. The government's objective was to produce teachers who would obey at command. Thus the school was operated like an army camp. Students were not allowed to leave the school grounds and dormitory area except on Saturday afternoon and Sunday. If they did leave, they were required to be back by 5:00 P.M. Newspapers were forbidden. Each day after the evening meal there was a two-hour study period during which complete silence was observed. As some students remember the experience, one could not open a desk drawer or even sneeze during this period.[4]

In this ambiance Makiguchi was made head of a boys' dormitory in 1900. In the spring of 1901 discipline in the dormitory came close to breaking down, but the extent to which Makiguchi was responsible for this is not clear. A key incident occurred during an annual military training field trip that involved all boys in the school with the exception of the fourth-year class. At one point in the course of the training maneuvers the students of a Lieutenant Nakamura, an instructor in military science, were given liberty with instructions to be back at the camp by 9:00 P.M. These students, however, apparently in a concerted act of defiance, did not report back to the camp until the next day. As a result the entire training exercise was thrown into a state of confusion and disorder. Although Makiguchi had not accompanied the students on the trip, he was considered officially responsible for this and other evidences of a breakdown of discipline among the students and was asked to resign.[5]

Makiguchi regretted the situation that led to his leaving Sapporo Normal School. At the same time, he had longed to have the opportunity to finish his geography manuscript, and as indicated earlier, the situation afforded the chance he needed to make the move to Tokyo. Thus it was that the summer of 1901 found Makiguchi, with his wife, two children, and a wicker basket stuffed with pages of his precious manuscript, making his way to Tokyo. Satoshi Ikeda describes the episode in these words: "The same restless energy that drove Makiguchi to Hokkaido when he was fourteen or fifteen now drove him to further pioneering. He was approaching middle age. He had no plan for the future, but he did have a wife, two children, and a manuscript."[6]

———————————————— *Makiguchi and the Academics*

In order to appreciate Makiguchi's position at this time, one must understand that in Japanese academic circles his normal-school education was not considered to be college- or university-level work. Among the scholars of his time Makiguchi was simply a lowly grammar school teacher. As such, without a university diploma, recognition as a competent scholar was forever lost to him. The one possible exception to this general rule was that of publishing. If he could publish a valuable piece of scholarly work, there would be some chance of gaining a reputation as a scholar.

While Makiguchi's motivation was probably to some extent simply due to a desire to be recognized, he also felt deeply that he had something important to say and he wanted to be heard. He was overjoyed, therefore, when he found some reputable scholars in Tokyo who were willing to listen to him. One of them was Kumezo Tsuboi, a young and energetic professor of history at Tokyo University. Although Makiguchi had no references and many questions, Professor Tsuboi went to considerable lengths to be helpful and to encourage Makiguchi in his writing. Shortly after moving to Tokyo, Makiguchi also made contact with Shigetaka Shiga, a widely recognized geographer whose book, *Nihon Fukeiron,* had first suggested to Makiguchi the idea of writing a book himself. Early in 1903 he took a six-inch-thick manuscript to Shiga and asked for criticism and guidance. Shiga, too, was impressed and said he would be glad to help. The encouragement of such men as Tsuboi and Shiga gave wings to Makiguchi's hopes. He plunged into his work with renewed vigor. By late summer the manuscript was ready for the publisher and in October it came off the press under the title *Jinsei Chirigaku* (The Geography of Human Life).

Initially Makiguchi had intended to entitle his book *Shakai Chirigaku* (Social Geography). However, at this time the political climate in Japan was such that even mention of the word *shakai* (society) carried the implication of *shakaishugi* (socialism), a word that meant treason to government authorities. Accordingly, the reluctant Makiguchi was persuaded by friends who "feared misunderstanding by ignorant and stubborn authorities" to change the title to *Jinsei Chirigaku.*[7]

The book was well received and considered by some scholars as a milestone in the development of the study of geography in Japan.[8] It was even recognized by the government and became the standard reference in geography for students preparing to take the government examination for teachers. Furthermore, the publication of the book brought Makiguchi into contact with scholars whom he otherwise might not have had the opportunity to meet. Included among them were Kunio Yanagida and Inazo Nitobe, two young scholars who were interested in the study of people and society. For a time Makiguchi was a part of a small group of intellectuals who gathered at Nitobe's home for discussion and debate. These two men, particularly Yanagida, were instrumental in launching Makiguchi into his next major interest and area of study: *kyodoka*, the study of local folk communities.

Although *Jinsei Chirigaku* was a significant contribution to Japanese education and scholarship and the acclaim Makiguchi received as a result of its publication notwithstanding, it did not serve to increase materially either his social standing or his financial resources. Kiyoaki Murata indicates that as a result of the success of his book Makiguchi wanted to make a career as a geographer, but he was apparently dissuaded from this course by the coolness of academic circles toward his aspirations.[9] The birth of a fifth child in 1907 brought the family to desperate financial straits. During the years following the publication of his book, Makiguchi tried various types of employment. He worked in a publishing office producing materials for high school teachers, edited a girls' magazine, and with an acquaintance, attempted to develop a correspondence school for girls. This last venture failed after two years. At one point he earned some money through a part-time job with the Ministry of Education editing geography texts.

The hardship and deprivation of these years left their mark on Makiguchi's personality. Satoshi Ikeda discusses at some length the probable effects of Makiguchi's early experiences on the development of his personality.[10] He believes there is no doubt that the formative years spent in the rugged, desolate country surrounding Arahama had something to do with Makiguchi's thinking about geography and its relationship to human life. Likewise, Ikeda believes that the poverty Makiguchi shared with his fellow students at Sapporo Normal School contributed to his deep feeling and concern for the poor and underprivileged.

Makiguchi's intense feeling for the poor and his conclusion that only among the common people could he find meaning and authenticity were very likely reinforced by his experiences during the years following publication of *Jinsei Chirigaku*. The struggles he endured during these years also forced Makiguchi to face the reality of his relationship to the university-educated elite of Japanese society. Thus in his later writings one finds references to the naiveté of the theoreticians who sit in their ivory towers with no conception of the problems faced by practical educators, i.e., classroom teachers. He called teachers to throw off the yoke that the theoreticians had forged for them and to develop their own sound pedagogy based on their experience as teachers.

Public School Teacher and Principal

The year 1909 brought Makiguchi more permanent work as a teacher at the Fujimi Primary School in Tokyo. After one year of teaching, however, he resigned due to ill health. Four months later, in August 1910, he had sufficiently regained his health to accept employment with the Ministry of Education to engage in a study and survey of local community cultures in selected parts of Japan. In 1913 he returned to active school work as principal of Tosei Primary School and for nearly two decades continued to serve as an elementary-school teacher and principal, sometimes both, in a series of schools in the Tokyo area. It was from random notes accumulated during this period of elementary-school work that Makiguchi's most significant work, *Soka Kyoikugaku Taikei* (The System of Value-Creating Pedagogy), later evolved.

Reference to official school records provides a general chronology of the schools where Makiguchi served. Based on his own research, Satoshi Ikeda gives a chronological history of Makiguchi's activities during this period. In addition, I personally reviewed and was permitted to photograph portions of the records of Shirogane Primary School, where Makiguchi served as principal from 1922 to 1928. More intimate and personal information about Makiguchi as a teacher and principal is difficult to obtain. It is possible to gain a coherent picture only by piecing together scattered impressions and views of Makiguchi's former students and others who were associated with him during this period. The picture that emerges is, first of all, one of a very studious person. Jiro Tokuda, a young teacher who taught at Shirogane Primary School during the years Makiguchi was principal, remembers that Makiguchi often worked in the teacher's room late into the night. In winter, he recalls, Makiguchi would put newspapers on his back under his kimono in order to keep warm as he sat working. All who knew him remember him as a very stern and dignified person. Yet many also remember him as a person who was extremely kind and deeply interested in individual students and their problems.

Makiguchi had deep convictions about the need to practice economy and thrift. Evidence that he practiced these traits in his own personal life is given by Kozaburo Nakabayashi when he writes that while younger teachers usually had several kimono, including white ones for summer, Makiguchi owned only one kimono, which he wore the year round. This was noticed even by the children at Taisho Primary School, who among themselves nicknamed Makiguchi *Fukuichi-chan* (one-suit man).

Both during his teaching and while engaged in community studies for the Ministry of Education from 1910 to 1913, the philosophical and pedagogical problems with which he had sought to deal in *Jinsei Chirigaku* remained uppermost in Makiguchi's mind. In the course of his study he had come in contact with the works of American and European sociologists and anthropologists. This may have come about as a result of his association with Yanagida and Nitobe, both of whom were pioneers in initiating sociological and anthropological studies in Japan. At any rate, Makiguchi's research in the area of community studies led to the publication in 1912 of a second book, *Kyodoka Kenkyu* (Research Studies in Folk Culture). In this volume the concepts of *Jinsei Chirigaku* were further developed and expanded in terms of the life and structures of local communities. Again, as in the earlier work, Makiguchi's chief concern was with the educational implications of studies in folk culture of local communities.

Makiguchi's persistent protest against the favoritism and special privilege enjoyed by the upper layers of Japan's stratified society was characteristic of his personality. In 1919, for example, he was dismissed from the position of principal of Taisho Primary School as the result of a petition initiated by the assistant principal and signed by many teachers and parents. The reason given for dismissal had to do with alleged misuse of funds given, according to Nakabayashi, by the mayor of Tokyo on the occasion of the opening of the school, funds for which Makiguchi as principal had been responsible. Though admittedly viewing the situation through the eyes of a student who idolized Makiguchi, Nakabayashi questions whether there had been any misuse of funds on Makiguchi's part. Rather, he believes, it was Makiguchi's attitude toward wealthy families and his refusal to show the least degree of favoritism to the children of wealthy families that was at the root of the dismissal. Makiguchi vigorously discouraged the common practice of teachers visiting the homes of only those children whose families were well to do.

Nakabayashi remembers vividly an incident in which wealthy parents requested special treatment of some kind for their daughter, who was a student in Taisho Primary School. Instead of complying, however, Makiguchi returned the gift that the girl's parents had sent to him. On such matters of principle he was adamant. Thus, while Makiguchi was generally considered an effective teacher and educator by the administrative authorities, such disregard for nearly sacred aspects of Japanese culture resulted in his being in constant conflict with the authorities, with fellow teachers, with parents, or with all three. Evidently it was just such incidents that built up over the years and led to his forced retirement from active school work in 1929. The manner of Makiguchi's retirement from active school work is interesting because of its subtlety. In 1928 he was transferred from Shirogane Primary School to Niibori Primary School in Azabu, a school that was scheduled to be closed the following year. This was equivalent to dismissal with a year's notice, a quiet means of getting rid of both Makiguchi and the troublesome issues that inevitably arose wherever he happened to be.*

After his transfer to the Niibori school, Makiguchi set himself the task of preparing for publication the educational ideas and methods that he had developed during his years of teaching. In the work of editing his notes Makiguchi found an invaluable assistant and ally in Josei Toda, a young school teacher from Hokkaido whom Makiguchi had assisted in obtaining a teaching position in 1920, when Makiguchi was principal of Nishimachi Primary School in Tokyo. Concerning Toda, Makiguchi wrote in 1930: "Since the writing was done at random, editing was a big job. Without the help of other people, particularly [Josei] Toda, who used my methods in his school and found them helpful, the work could never have been done. In fact, Mr. Toda became so enthusiastic that it seems as if he were the initiator and I the follower."[11] Toda continued to work closely with his revered teacher until both were arrested in 1943.

Makiguchi envisioned a twelve-volume work that was to be entitled, as indicated earlier, *Soka Kyoikugaku Taikei*. The first volume was published in 1930, the second in 1931, the third in 1932, and the fourth in 1934; however, the eight subsequent volumes were never published. It is interesting to note that ten years elapsed between the publication of the fourth volume and Makiguchi's death in 1944. Why, one may wonder, did he not produce additional volumes of his proposed work during this ten-year period? A possible explanation may be that Maki-

---

*There is lack of agreement as to the date of the closing of the Niibori School. Kiyoaki Murata gives the 1929 date, whereas Satoshi Ikeda and the March, 1971, issue of *Todai* cite it as 1932.

guchi's own views were undergoing change during this period as a result of his conversion to the Nichiren Shoshu sect of Japanese Buddhism in 1928. This religious interest, it would appear, led to the rearrangement of some of his objectives and priorities and involved him in activities that consumed his time and energy, thus turning his attention away from later volumes of his proposed work.

Sources of Makiguchi's Educational Ideas

Soka Gakkai claims that the origin and basis of Makiguchi's thought lay in the doctrine of Nichiren Shoshu. In a general sense this is true, but the claim leaves a number of important things unsaid. First of all, Makiguchi was not converted to Nichiren Shoshu until 1928. This was just one year before his forced retirement from active school work. He had already spent nearly four decades in some type of educational work, as either teacher or administrator or in research and writing of educational materials. By this time Makiguchi's basic concepts and ideas had been formulated. It is my conclusion, based on both examination of historical materials and interviews with people who were closely associated with Makiguchi, that not until several years after his conversion, during the mid-1930s, did Nichiren Shoshu doctrine come to be an important element in his thought. If this is an accurate assessment of the data, it would mean that Nichiren Shoshu doctrine had not significantly influenced Makiguchi's thought during the time he compiled and edited his major work, *Soka Kyoikugaku Taikei,* roughly from 1929 to 1933. In fact the basic concepts of Makiguchi's system, the philosophy of value and value creation, are present in embryonic form in *Jinsei Chirigaku,* which he published in

1903—many years before his relationship with Nichiren Shoshu began.

Makiguchi's educational thought and practice, then, may legitimately be considered in two parts. The first is the philosophy and pedagogy that developed from his nearly forty years as a professional educator, which is considered in the next chapter and is summarized in the four completed volumes of *Soka Kyoikugaku Taikei*. The second is the thought and practice that grew out of his efforts to integrate this earlier work in education with Nichiren Shoshu doctrine, which is manifested in Soka Gakkai. The influence of Nichiren Shoshu doctrine on Makiguchi's thinking and the religious movement that developed from that ideological union are discussed in chapter four.

Before considering these two facets of Makiguchi's educational thought and practice, one should explore the intellectual sources of the educational ideas contained in *Soka Kyoikugaku Taikei*. "From perusing various published works, from reading newspapers and magazines, from listening to the conversation of businessmen, from nature, from observing people, in other words, in response to necessity and according to feeling and experience, I made notes that accumulated to make a small volume."[12] Thus Makiguchi described the sources of his educational ideas. Interestingly he did not in his writings, with one or two exceptions, acknowledge a debt to specific individuals or philosophical schools. On the contrary, he strongly emphasized that his ideas and practices in education grew out of his own experience. He was particularly quick to deny dependence on Western scholars and educators. Makiguchi must be clearly understood here because, as a matter of fact, it is possible to identify with some degree of certainty the major ideological sources of influence in the development of his thought, and many of them were Western sources. What he meant was that he did not slavishly or unthinkingly depend upon or accept the views of particular Western scholars. Rather, he insisted, every educational idea or method must be put to the acid test of actual educational practice. Those ideas that proved valid and useful in practice were to be accepted and incorporated into one's own educational practice. Those ideas that did not so prove themselves were to be discarded.

A cursory examination of Makiguchi's writings suggests that he must have been an avid reader of the works of both Japanese and Western scholars. The list of people cited in his writings is impressive. With reference to Western scholars there is scarcely a single major figure in the fields of education and social science, from the time of Plato to the early decades of the twentieth century, to whose work he did not make some reference. However, despite this wide acquaintance with scholarly works, there were actually three main sources of the ideas that influenced the development of Makiguchi's educational philosophy and pedagogy. One of these, the study of geography, was considered above. The second was the educational school of pragmatism, including its European predecessors, of which John Dewey was the chief spokesman.

That Dewey's early writings were a major resource for Makiguchi is evident from an examination of his *Soka Kyoikugaku Taikei*. However, at that time the language barrier ruled out the possibility of effective two-way communication between Makiguchi and Dewey. Dewey died probably without ever hearing of Makiguchi. It is well known, of course, that Dewey lectured in Japan in 1919, spending more than two and a half months there, from February 9 to April 28. However, there is no evidence that Makiguchi met Dewey at that time or that they could have conversed if they had met. On the contrary, evidence suggests that personal communication with Dewey was difficult and limited. Research conducted by Victor Kobayashi reveals that Dewey's lectures were delivered in English without the aid of an interpreter. Kobayashi believes that it was primarily this inability to communicate effectively with Japanese educators that caused attendance to dwindle from about seven hundred people at Dewey's first lecture to less than one hundred at his eighth and final lecture.[13]

The third source of influence on Makiguchi's educational thought stemmed from the concepts of modern sociology and anthropology that he became enamored of during the years following the publication of *Jinsei Chirigaku*. Here the works of Lester Ward seemed especially to challenge him. In addition to evidence of Ward's influence in *Soka Kyoikugaku Taikei*, including references to both Ward's books and his major concepts, people who were close to Makiguchi have attested to the importance Ward's writings had for Makiguchi. One such person is Shuhei Yajima, a member of the central leadership of Soka Kyoiku Gakkai from 1935 until his arrest with Makiguchi in 1943. During an interview Yajima stated that Ward's writings had served as a major philosophical grounding for Makiguchi's thought. He also stressed the importance of the influence of Dewey's writings, but he insisted that Makiguchi's philosophy of value went beyond the educational pragmatism of Dewey because Dewey failed to make the distinction between truth and value.

If one considers the mixture of these three lines of thought— the importance of the learner's geographic environment to the educational process, the emphasis on experience and the scientific method stemming from the pragmatic orientation, and the recognition of education's sociological dimensions—all within the particular context in which Makiguchi worked, it is possible to discern the broad outlines of the educational philosophy and pedagogy that issued from his thought and work.

3 Value-Creating Pedagogy

Japanese Miseducation

"Japanese education," Makiguchi wrote in 1930, "is haphazard, unplanned, fragmented, and purposeless."[1] This kind of education he designated as "natural education." Natural education, according to Makiguchi, had grown up as a result of teachers unthinkingly collecting every manner of educational theory and practice from here, there, and everywhere, particularly from the West. Despite the fact that there were numerous contradictions among these theories and practices and although teachers for the most part did not understand any of them, they attempted to add them all together to make up what was supposed to be children's education.

Makiguchi did not devote time to systematic description of the Japanese educational system about which he was so critical. Accordingly, one has to rely on other sources for this information.* The educational picture that emerges from such study is of a fixed curriculum of orderly subject matter, based partially on the past and partially on the newly introduced scientific subjects of the West, which children were expected to master through drill and repetition. On top of this there had been added a superficial overlay of various progressive educational reforms, which were limited primarily to the area of teaching methods. For example, Japanese educators' interest in Dewey prior to World War II was limited to methods of teaching, according to Kobayashi. He asserts that prior to this time there were few if any educators in Japan who grasped the deeper aspects of Dewey's educational philosophy.[2]

Makiguchi believed that the result of the kind of education described above was disastrous. He claimed that under these conditions the educational experiences of children consisted of little more than mental gymnastics and memorization of material unrelated to their lives. This kind of education did more harm than good to the rising generation. Furthermore, the loss both to the children and to the nation lay not only in what was happening to children taught in this way; equally important was what failed to happen. The great potential of each child was not being developed or nurtured. Makiguchi

*For further information in this area, see Herbert Passin, *Society and Education in Japan* (New York: Columbia University, Teachers College, Bureau of Publications, 1965).

credited the lack of development of this potential in children to "the pitiful and tragic conditions in which many people live."[3] His desire "to save the children of Japan from being victimized by the deplorable inadequacies of traditional Japanese education and to assure that oncoming generations of Japanese children will not have to suffer its devastations"[4] became the consuming passion and central motivation of Makiguchi's life.

As an alternative to natural education Makiguchi suggested and drew up the outline for what he called "cultural education." By this he meant an educational system intentionally developed according to rational, logical, and scientific criteria to achieve clearly defined purposes. We will consider the implications of cultural education, or value-creating pedagogy, as Makiguchi preferred to describe his proposed system of education. First, however, we must examine the educational philosophy out of which value-creating pedagogy emerged.

A Philosophy of Education

Philosophy and educational philosophy were one and the same to Makiguchi. Philosophy for him centered in a theory of value creation. In his major work, *Soka Kyoikugaku Taikei, so,* which means creation, and *ka,* which means value, form a key word and a key concept. Creation of value is part and parcel of what it means to be a human being. Human beings do not have the ability to create material; but they can create value, and it is in the creation of value that the unique meaning of human life lies. Makiguchi further elaborated his philosophy in terms of human happiness. "The highest and ultimate object of life," he held, "is happiness, and the goal of life is none but the attainment and creation of value, which is in itself happiness. . . . A happy life signifies nothing but the state of existence in which one can gain and create value in full."[5]

Makiguchi insisted that his theory of value creation could not be comprehended even in the slightest without a correct knowledge of value. He sought to make explicit what he meant by value through contrasting it with truth. Noah Brannen, one of the few Western scholars who has studied Makiguchi's writings, has very ably summarized this aspect of Makiguchi's thought: "Makiguchi's theory claims to be a correction of the alleged aberrations of the traditional platonic values—truth, goodness, and beauty—by the substitution of 'benefit'* for that of 'truth.' The reason for this is said to be that truth and value are entirely different concepts. Truth reveals that which is; value connotes a subject-object relationship. Truth makes epistemological statements about an object. Value relates the object to man. Truth says, 'Here is a horse'; value says, 'The horse is beautiful.' "[6]

Truth, according to Makiguchi's philosophy, cannot be created; it remains always as that which is, that which is discovered. He held that value, however, can be created. Creation involves changing the ordinary order of nature into a special one through human activity, increasing its usefulness for human life. Clarification of this aspect of Makiguchi's thought can be gained by referring to Ward's writings. In 1888, for example, Ward wrote: "Man can make very little use of anything in its natural state. Value, i.e., utility, is imparted to raw materials only by labor and skill. The products of labor and skill are artificial, and scarcely anything has *actual* value, i.e., capability of actual, immediate use, until it has

---

*Note that Brannen translates the Japanese word *ri* as benefit. This word can also be translated as gain. The latter translation, which is officially used by Soka Gakkai, is employed throughout this book with the exception of quoted passages.

been transformed from the natural into the artificial state. Therefore, if that which can be used is superior to that which cannot, the artificial is superior to the natural."[7] Makiguchi further held that truth never changes, whereas values do.[8] In this respect Makiguchi was very much a relativist. During his career as an educator he consistently rejected the idea of absolute values.

An important aspect of value creation for Makiguchi was the development of a harmonious balance between individual and social values. On one hand, he stressed that an action by an individual that brings gain to himself could be an evil to the society of which he is a member. On the other, Makiguchi held not only that working for gain is an entirely proper and honorable pursuit, but that it is a responsibility of each individual, as a creator of value, to work for gain in such a way as to contribute to the welfare of both himself and his society. This is a central element in Makiguchi's thought and comes clearly into focus as one examines the distinctions that he perceived among the three elements of value. Thus beauty is perceived to be an emotional and temporary value, derived through one or more of the five senses, that concerns only a part of man's life. Gain is an individual value that is related to the whole of man's life. It has to do with the relationship between an individual and an object that contributes to the maintenance and development of his life. Goodness, however, is a social value related to the life of the group. It refers to the personal conduct of an individual that intentionally contributes to the formation and development of a unified society. Goodness is public gain.[9] The person who understands the difference between truth and value and the distinctions among the various elements of value will seek a harmonious balance between the pursuit of the values of gain and good. The development of people possessing these capabilities is a central task of education according to Makiguchi's view.

The antitheses of beauty, gain, and good are ugliness, loss, and evil. "Value means the total amount of force with which an object (be it material or spiritual) causes a subject to attain its purpose as the means to an end. It is called good, gain, or beauty according to each kind and degree of value that is considered to be favorable to the maintenance of human existence, which is the aim of life. Furthermore, these kinds of value are summarized by such words as 'valuable,' 'of much value,' or 'of little value.' However, value is called evil, loss, or ugliness according to the kind and degree to which it is recognized as being harmful to the maintenance of life."[10] Makiguchi continued: "When we consider the phenomena of the external world, we can divide them into two kinds: those that bear positive usefulness to human existence and those that are harmful. Thus, evil vs. good, loss vs. gain, and ugliness vs. beauty represent the negative side of human life." Makiguchi insisted that these negative values should be thought of as " 'antivalue' rather than 'nonexistent value.' " This is because while "antivalue cannot be called beauty, gain, or good, it likewise cannot be called nonvalue, because its presence sometimes exerts a great influence on the evaluating subject."[11]

Makiguchi also stressed the importance of distinguishing between cognition and evaluation. "Considering the present situation of the world, I believe nothing is so evil as the confusion of cognition and evaluation, since mixing the two makes comprehension difficult for a person and causes him to assume an uncertain attitude toward his choice and decision. Even among leading intellectuals, this confusion of cognition and evaluation is observed in their everyday conversation. They are unaware of it, discuss matters without knowing their causes, and arbitrarily pass judgment according to their likes and dislikes. . . . These people are misled in their ways of thinking and acting."[12]

As an example of this kind of confusion, Makiguchi writes:

"Suppose a pupil asks his teacher: 'What is this?' If the teacher scolds him and says: 'Do you mean to say you still don't know what it is?' he is definitely confusing the processes of cognition and evaluation. The pupil who asked the question was not asking for a judgment on his own competence. He was seeking information. The teacher who does not answer the pupil's real question but diverts his attention to something else is intimidating the child. If he thinks he is helping the child's comprehension he is mistaken. . . . With a teacher of this kind, a poor pupil cannot help becoming an even poorer pupil."[13] This kind of confusion can be observed, Makiguchi wrote, "in every class of society—in governmental offices, trading companies, and the factories of minor enterprises. . . . In actuality, the confusion of cognition and evaluation has been forcing the world into various chaotic conditions."[14]

But what specifically must one comprehend in order to avoid this confusion? What is the distinction between cognition and evaluation that one must understand? Brannen's analysis of Makiguchi's answer to this question can scarcely be improved upon: "Evaluation is the consciousness of the influence of an object upon the subject. Cognition is the grasping of the meaning of an impression. Evaluation, therefore, is subjective; cognition is objective. For example, cognition asserts 'A is B,' or 'A is not C.' Thus cognition receives an object as it is without relating it to the subject. Evaluation, on the other hand, says 'A is beautiful,' etc., and relates it to the evaluating subject.

"Cognition, therefore, is concerned with truth while evaluation is concerned with values. Truth is a qualitative concept grasped by intellectual response to the stimuli of phenomena; that is, by cognition. Value is a quantitative concept relating the influence of phenomena to man through emotional and intellectual responses; that is, by evaluation. Cognition is mental reception or intellectual activity; evaluation is sense reception or feeling activity.

"Cognition comes by the relation of a new perception to a past experience. Kant says that man perceives by *a priori* standards; but the truth is that man first decides whether something is the 'same or different' on the basis of his experience. It isn't necessary to adopt the method of some philosopher (such as Kant) when we have the time-tested method of 'same or different.'

"The relation of cognition to external phenomena we call 'experience.' This term experience is defined to mean the sensual, intellectual connection of subject and object. The relation of evaluation to external phenomena we call 'intercourse.' Intercourse is defined as the emotional, sentimental connection of subject and object. In the case of the former, the external world has its independent existence and is not directly connected with our personal world. In the case of the latter, the external world has a vital, intimate connection with our world."[15]

Thus, in order to know the external world, both cognition and evaluation are essential according to Makiguchi. Understanding is incomplete if either is neglected. Man faces a serious problem in the modern world because science has pursued the objective method of cognition and has analyzed and classified phenomena until we are left with only the pieces. However, Makiguchi maintained that cognition and evaluation do not need to be in conflict. They may appear to conflict in describing phenomena, but this is a conflict arising out of the opposition of the whole to the parts and is not a basic conflict.

The accuracy of Makiguchi's insights in this regard and his grasp of the learning process are being verified today by competent educators. George I. Brown, for example, cites the traditional tendency in American education for teachers to focus on the cognitive elements in learning and to neglect the affective elements as the most critical problem facing educators today.* Similarly, Michael Novak writes that American schools "are not characteristically interested in the depth of their students' fantasy life, the complexity of their emotions, the delicacy of their sensitivity, the variety and range of their instincts—only in their capacity to store information and to analyze information."[16]

Two other educators have recently commented on the problems created by the general tendency to confuse expressions of fact and expressions of value. Theodore Brameld writes that the "trouble arises from the fact that neither kind of value judgment [i.e., characterizing and appraising] is clearly perceived or differentiated in everyday educational experience. Rather, both characterizing and appraising value judgments are usually made haphazardly, half-consciously if not unconsciously, and even contradictorily by teachers, administrators, parents, students, and citizens in general."[17] David J. Bond writes that the "new education" of recent years is no less ineffective than the traditional accumulation-of-knowledge type of education that it replaced because "we make either the wrong or no distinctions between statements of fact, expressions of feeling, moral judgments, aesthetic preferences, value claims, and nonsense noises."[18]

The confusion of truth and value and of cognition and evaluation has implications for experimentation and the experimental method. Thus, Makiguchi wrote, truth "can be proved by confronting it with a fact, i.e., by making an abstract concept concrete and experimenting to determine whether or not the expression agrees with the one that has been realized. However, value cannot be proved merely through such intellectual reasoning. Between object and subject there is relative force and in proving value there is no method other than proving through experiment the influence an object

*See his book *Human Teaching for Human Learning: An Introduction to Confluent Education* (New York: Viking Press, 1971).

exerts on the subject that evaluates it."[19] Makiguchi was critical of Western pragmatism precisely at this point. In confusing
truth with value and treating them as being alike and equal,
Western pragmatism, he contended, makes the false assumption
that if a thing is true it is beneficial to man. Experience does
not support such an assumption. On the contrary, experience
tells us that some things that have no usefulness to human life
are true.[20]

As indicated earlier, the highest and ultimate object of human life for Makiguchi was happiness. This aspect of his philosophy can be easily misunderstood and may perhaps need some
further discussion. Happiness, as Makiguchi used the word,
does not refer to some nebulous emotional state that may be
implied by either the English word or the Japanese word
(*kofuku*) of which it is a translation. Happiness, as used by
Makiguchi, refers to a state of man's life when he is engaged
in the process of attaining and creating value.

If one thinks a little bit, Makiguchi suggested, one knows
that happiness cannot be gained by oneself, nor can it be inherited like property. People with money and property think
they can inherit happiness, as well. They become eager to gain
more and more money and property. But happiness, as Alfred
Bernhard Nobel wrote, cannot be inherited like property. If
everyone recognized this, there would be no reason for conflict between capitalists and labor, for war, and so forth.[21]

Education is the means whereby the members of a society
acquire competence as creators of value and thus find happiness. Not the happiness of the parents, Makiguchi insisted,
but the happiness of the educated. Parents should not, as he
observed they were doing, use the educated to fulfill their own
happiness. This is what Makiguchi meant when he wrote that
happiness is the aim of education.[22] But happiness has two elements: personal and social. When some scholars, such as Kant,
object that happiness is not adequate as the aim of education,

Makiguchi states that it is because they see only the personal element of happiness. If Kant had known of the sociology of Comte, he might have accepted happiness as the aim of education. It is quite natural for us to reject happiness as the aim of education if the social element is omitted. However, now that we know of sociology, Makiguchi believed, the objection to happiness as the aim of education ought to disappear.[23]

When Makiguchi stated, then, that education is the means whereby individuals can acquire competence as creators of value, and thereby find happiness in the process, he was taking it for granted that this dual personal-social nature of man is understood. The educated person in these terms, as noted earlier, is one who recognizes the tension between the values of gain and good in his life and seeks a harmonious balance between them in the decisions that he makes. This means, further, that the educated person senses and accepts responsibility both for his own life and for the society of which he is a part. A major theme running through Makiguchi's educational philosophy is that the educational systems that he knew were not capable of educating individuals in this way, i.e., individuals prepared to be creators of both personal gain and social good. To provide education of this kind would require a pedagogy specifically designed to accomplish the desired objectives. Such a pedagogy would have to be based on the philosophy of value and the concept of value creation and would have to meet tests of scientific or logical practicability.

Implications and Applications

Makiguchi's major criticism of the educational practice of his day was that it was built in the clouds with no basis in experience. "There are two main streams of thought in the educational world. One consists of the empiricists, who emphasize experience, the other consists of the theorists, who emphasize philosophical thinking. Those who are engaged in actual teaching belong to the empiricist stream, and since there are two hundred thousand teachers, they could have made excellent manuscripts of teaching methods, if they had tried. In actuality, however, the theorists, who import many kinds of educational theories and pedagogies from Europe, hold over-whelming power and control over the empiricists, or actual educators."[24] Makiguchi went on to say that the theorists, in introducing new ideas from Europe, employ the deductive method, which begins with theory or abstract philosophy. The ideas and conclusions of the theorists, deductively arrived at, are worthless in actual teaching.

In other writings Makiguchi discussed the same problem in terms of two ways of studying education. One is philosophical pedagogy, the other scientific pedagogy. By the latter he meant a "pedagogy that faces necessity and develops pedagogy to meet needs."[25] Makiguchi, of course, considered his own value-creating pedagogy as a scientific pedagogy. Makiguchi insisted that teachers should no longer let the theorists, with their abstract philosophical thinking, have the control and initiative in the educational world. Rather, teachers should reflect upon their own teaching experiences, inducing principles from them, and cease to worry about the conflicting things that the theorists, who are far away from actual teaching, have to say.

The advancement of education, therefore, and indeed the establishment of a scientific pedagogy depend in Makiguchi's view on the use of the inductive method by actual teachers. What such teachers have to do "is to affirm cases of success and failure by analyzing their daily teaching experiences, and then they will find valuable truths."[26] This inductive method, which, Makiguchi asserted, is actually the method of scientific inquiry, was introduced by Francis Bacon and is the only way to advance the educational world. Later, Comenius explored the implications of the scientific method for teaching, and educators have been talking about a scientific pedagogy ever since, but talking is all they have done. Thus Makiguchi contended that although it is now several centuries after the explorations of these early educational pioneers, we still have not developed a truly scientific pedagogy.

To emphasize his assertion that educators had failed to avail themselves of the benefits and possibilities of scientific inquiry, Makiguchi contrasted the state of education with that of medicine. Educators, he suggested, can only be described as groping in the dark, whereas in the medical world practicing physicians assemble to report their experiences, as well as to hear reports of great scholars and read the translations of foreign works. The physicians are making great progress, Makiguchi asserted. Although medicine and pedagogy belong to the same field of applied science, the field that deals with the lives of human beings, there is a great difference in the development of the two. The reason for this is that medicine has been firmly established as an applied science.[27]

As Makiguchi saw it, the new pedagogy could thus come from only one source: "Actual educators should look back over fifty years of experience and search for effective methods of teaching."[28] That he was pessimistic about the possibility of a pedagogy thus derived being generally accepted is suggested by his statement: "If I, only a primary school principal, try to make up a new pedagogy, educators might laugh at me and say that it is a task for those scholars who understand foreign languages."[29] On one occasion, Makiguchi wrote, he "was told by a government official responsible for supervising education: 'Why don't you experiment with new kinds of pedagogy after you retire?' "[30] However, such apprehensions and open discouragement did not deter him from working at the task, as his *Soka Kyoikugaku Taikei* evidences.

The pedagogy that evolved in the early 1930s, as Makiguchi looked back over his own experience of nearly forty years in education, was characterized by two main features that set it in contrast to current educational practice of the time. First of all, in Makiguchi's pedagogy, heavy emphasis was given to educational purpose and the integration, not only of curriculum, but of all learning experiences in terms of purpose. This purpose, as noted above, centered in the concept of value creation. The valuable personality, the happy person, is the person who has great ability to create value. The purpose of education, therefore, is to increase the value creativity of the educated. What *soka* (value creating) pedagogy seeks to do, Makiguchi wrote in 1930, "is to find and make clear the methods to accomplish this aim."[31] This cultural objective would be at the heart of an adequate educational system and would bring unity and integration to the educational experience provided for the young. Secondly, and closely related to the first, Makiguchi envisioned an educational system that would be socially responsible. These two predominant characteristics of Makiguchi's pedagogy are caught up in two terms that appear frequently in his writings, *bunka kyoiku* (cultural education) and *kyodoka* (community study).

The word kyodoka has meanings that are not adequately reflected by "community study." The Japanese word carries a connotation signifying that the local community is one in which a person has a definite stake. It signifies that a person is intimately related to the community by virtue of residence in it. When related to pedagogical concerns, the community becomes the interconnected network of personal and structural relationships that occur in the geographic area in which one's life is sustained. Makiguchi saw more clearly and exploited more fully than perhaps any other educator the pedagogical possibilities in that network of relationships.

If cultural education may be said to express the overall aim of education for Makiguchi, community study expresses its central method. Community study was an extension and refinement of his earlier work in geography, an extension and refinement based on his discovery of sociology and sociological concepts. Through study of the community, the hometown or neighborhood, Makiguchi believed that children can observe directly the complex relationships between land and life, between nature and society. By this means the educator can help students understand the meaning and significance of home, school, and city or village. Moreover, this lays the foundation for establishing ties with the nation and the world.

Community study was for Makiguchi the basic starting point of all study and courses; and not only the starting point but the destination, as well. This means that students, rather than studying the traditional subjects, such as history, geography, mathematics, and so forth, study life by means of the insights and concepts offered by the various academic subjects and disciplines. The traditional pattern of teaching fragmented, unrelated subject matter is uneconomical and ineffective. Such isolated subject matter is dead knowledge because of its unrelatedness to children's lives. When community study is made the central unifying and integrating focus of children's educational experience, it becomes possible to relate things taught to the actual life of a community of people and to the social, economic, and political structures of the community. Such knowledge is living knowledge; and only living knowledge is useful knowledge, Makiguchi insisted.

One of Makiguchi's central concerns was that children should begin, from their earliest educational experience, to acquire a deep understanding and awareness of the structures, first of all, of their local community and then of the larger national

and world communities. The development of such understanding and awareness of the structures of the social body was,
for Makiguchi, the very essence of the educational task. "To
study many other subjects without studying the total society,"
Makiguchi wrote, "is like building a house on sand." Studying
the nature and cultural cohesiveness of a total society, Makiguchi believed, helps to give direction to the study of other
subjects.[32] Only people who grasp the meaning and significance of social life would be able to live effectively and com-
petently in a scientifically oriented world. Furthermore, only
such people can be creators of value in the fullest sense. The
great tragedy of education as Makiguchi saw it was that education, fragmented and unrelated to life as it had been,
traditionally gave children only a superficial veneer of understanding of life in society, which was almost worse than no
education at all.

It is clear in Makiguchi's writings that he was completely
egalitarian in his view of human potential. He was vehemently
opposed to the view that only highly gifted natures, after an
elitist form of educational experience, can acquire the comprehensive grasp of life and society that he advocated. Every
normal person, he insisted, is a potential creator of value and
is potentially a skilled participant in the life of his community
and his world. Whether or not such potential is developed
depends largely on the kind of educational experience provided
by society.

Makiguchi recognized that the kind of educational experience he advocated for children would be possible and
feasible only to the extent that competent teachers were available. Teachers who cannot comprehend the nature of the
teaching task, i.e., developing value-creating people—teachers
who do not themselves understand the structures of the society
in which they live—are unfit to be teachers. Yet, the reality
that Makiguchi faced was that Japanese teachers of his day

were, almost without exception, unfit by his standards. The improvement of teachers and teaching, therefore, became the primary means whereby he hoped to change Japanese education and society. "We have to start," he wrote in volume two of *Soka Kyoikugaku Taikei,* "by helping teachers comprehend the fundamental concepts of life, education, and society. Otherwise, we can never escape from the long-established customs and patterns of traditional education."[33] For teachers to try to learn mere techniques before acquiring this deeper comprehension is a waste of time. Nearly as important is that teachers cease to see their role as one of filling children full of knowledge, and see it instead as one of nurturing and developing the abilities and powers of children to think and study and acquire knowledge and understanding by their own initiative. The time would come, Makiguchi predicted, when teachers who cling to a style of teaching that seeks simply an accumulation of factual knowledge by the student would be in danger of losing their jobs.[34]

It is necessary, therefore, that teachers begin to define their role in other terms. A major aspect of this redefinition as Makiguchi saw it was a view of the teacher as leading children through the processes of discovery and invention, rather than filling them with accumulations of knowledge. This basic principle of learning, Makiguchi asserted, has been known to educators from the times of Comenius and Pestalozzi but has not affected the educational practice of teachers. The reason for this, he charged, was a failure upon the part of teachers to engage in study and research on their own initiative. On one occasion he observed that "the only time teachers study is when the Ministry of Education directs them to do so, or in order to pass a teacher's examination."[35]

This charge that teachers themselves were largely to blame for the sad state of children's education reveals the main thrust of Makiguchi's thinking in regard to teacher training.

While in his writings he occasionally referred to possibilities for official action and official programs that could be under-taken to upgrade the quality and effectiveness of Japanese teachers, he seemed never to have been overly optimistic as to their realization. Within the actualities of the Japanese cul-ture and government of his time, Makiguchi concluded that personal study and growth upon the part of individual teachers offered the best hope of educational improvement and reform. Accordingly, his efforts after his release from active school work in 1929 focused on the development of aids and resources to assist teachers in their own study and teaching.

Makiguchi's writings are filled with elaborate and detailed suggestions and illustrative examples to help teachers effectively utilize the methods and principles of community study. Of course some of the suggestions and illustrations in his writings are dated and would be inappropriate for present-day use. Furthermore, this material was prepared to be used in con-junction with text materials prescribed by the Ministry of Education. But such limitations notwithstanding, the material still provides insight into the concepts and principles of com-munity study as an educational experience as envisioned by Makiguchi. The following ideas and suggestions are illustrative of this material:

1. In every school system there are problems of order, regulations that must be made and obeyed if the life of the school is to go on. What if some students do not want to abide by the rules? This is politics. The wise teacher can take this living experience and help students learn basic concepts and principles of political life that will have application in national and world politics, as well as in their local community.

2. Similarly, such questions as these may be asked: Who pays the expenses of the school? What is the cost of constructing a school building? How much is the yearly budget? What is

1. Tsunesaburo Makiguchi in his late sixties, at the beginning of World War II.

2. *Makiguchi and his wife, Kuma.*

3. Makiguchi with a class at Shirogane Primary School in Tokyo, probably in 1924 or 1925.

4. *Participants in the 1937 meeting at the Tokyo restaurant Kikusuitei for the formal organization of Soka Kyoiku Gakkai. Makiguchi is seated in the center of the first row; Josei Toda is standing at the far right in the second row.*

5. *Makiguchi and members of the revolutionary cadre that gathered around him in the ▷ 1930s. Left to right: Shingi Shibuya, Doki (surname unknown), Makiguchi, Shuhei Yajima, and Tsutomu Watanabe, Makiguchi's son-in-law.*

6. *Josei Toda, Makiguchi's disciple and the second president of Soka Gakkai.*

7. *Daisaku Ikeda, Toda's disciple and the third president of Soka Gakkai.*

8. Soka High School.

9. Soka University.

創價教育學

牧口常三郎氏が教育に對する識見と熱烈なる努力によりて今日其の所の如き優秀なる實績を擧げられたるは、東京市白金小學校が全國一般の學校を凌ぎ金甌無缺の成績を物語るものにして、世間利を來むる所當世稀なる世の人の及ぶべからざるものなり。氏や人格を來め、善を積み惡を去り君子の德を總べて備へ、高潔なる紛々たる世を絶つ君子の努力をなせる所多し。

其の日常善を積み善を稱へ、獨り其の道を語り、其の敎育に盡すは、人格の完成のため到底他の企及するを許さず。更に數ふること能はず。思ふに先生の創價教育學は、積年の思索と實驗を經たる獨自の教育體系にして、其の教育體系の完成に、不斷之と肝膽を同じくし、其の功績の貴重なるを知り、之を欽仰してその後援の努力をなせんことに對し、支援會を興し以て之が後援の實を擧げんとするものである。氏に對し以て支援會ある所なり。

政友會總裁　犬養毅
民政黨總裁　濱口雄幸
前遞信大臣　望月圭介
前農林大臣　渡邊千冬
前文部大臣　牧野良三
前東京市長　柳田...
東京市助役　中...
東京市教育局長　前田米藏
東京市視學官　古島一雄
　　　　　　　安藤正純
　　　　　　　宅田...
　　　　　　　鳩山一郎
　　　　　　　田...
　　　　　　　山野...
　　　　　　　野田...
　　　　　　　戸...

法學博士　岸...
政學博士　野...
男爵　山田高人
醫學博士　中木修
貴族院議員　秋江...
商學博士　山...
工學博士　口...
工學博士　中松...
農學博士　水野...

東京市議會議員　渡間雄彦夫
　　　　　　　　本中...
改委員　木...
年...　孫...
會議員　稻田德...
土木技師　川...
　　　　　　　　野...
　　　　　　　　鎌一良...
　　　　　　　　太...

鎌田...　定五郎　清一郎　正一郎...

IN SUPPORT OF VALUE-CREATING PEDAGOGY

The remarkable achievements that Mr. Tsunesaburo Makiguchi has made in education, through his excellent insight and intense efforts, are so widely acknowledged that they need not be mentioned here. The meritorious record attained by the pupils of Shirogane Primary School is only one example of his many achievements.

Mr. Makiguchi is a man of lofty character. In a world in which most people take advantage of petty interests merely to seek their own glory, Mr. Makiguchi is unique in finding pleasure in persistent devotion to education.

In spite of the great pressure of his work, Mr. Makiguchi's own studies have never ceased. Indeed, he is outstanding among his colleagues because of his painstaking efforts and his wholehearted devotion to the complete systematization of his unique educational theory through the accumulation and application of his ceaseless cogitation and valuable teaching experience.

In recognition of his merits and with deep respect for his character, and to show our respect for his efforts toward the perfecting of his invaluable educational system, it is our duty, and is moreover a great privilege allowed those of us who know him, to extend him our moral support.

To this end we are herewith honored to establish this group to support Value-Creating Pedagogy.

Tsuyoshi Inukai, *President of Seiyukai (political party)*
Masahiro Ota, *Director, Kanto District Agency*
Inazo Nitobe, *Director of Law, Doctor of Agriculture*
Kazuo Kojima, *Former Vice-Minister of Communications*
Ichiro Hatoyama, *Former Chief Cabinet Secretary, Director of Seiyukai*
Masatake Nakano, *Vice-Minister of Communications*
Yonezo Maeda, *Former Director of the Legislative Bureau, Director of Seiyukai*
Yoshitaka Furuya, *Director of the Democratic Party*
Masazumi Ando, *Former Education Councilor*
Tamon Maeda, *Former Deputy Mayor of Tokyo*
Shotaro Miyake, *Supreme Court Judge*
Kunio Yanagida, *Former Chief Secretary of the House of Peers*
Ryozo Makino, *Member of the House of Representatives*
Chifuyu Watanabe, *Minister of Justice*
Rentaro Mizuno, *Former Minister of Education, Doctor of Law*

Kakuhei Matsuno, *Director of Seiyukai*
Yoshinaga Nakagawa, *Baron*
Ichiji Yamauchi, *Member of the House of Peers*
Teijo Eguchi, *Director of the Board of Mitsubishi Company, Director of Taihei Life Insurance Company*
Kiyoshi Akita, *Former Vice-Minister of Home Affairs, Director of Seiyukai*
Tokugoro Nakahashi, *Former Minister of Education, Commerce, and Industry*
Magoichi Tawara, *Minister of Commerce and Industry*
Takamasa Hachijo, *Viscount*
Itsuma Takagi, *Professor at the Imperial University, Doctor of Medicine*
Tatsuo Tanaka, *Doctor of Engineering*
Sanehiko Yamamoto, *President of Kaizo Company*
Kaneo Nomaguchi, *Admiral*
Fukuo Kishibe, *Member of Tokyo Municipal Assembly*

the major expense? What is tuition used for? From this direct recognition of the school's economic situation, not only can students learn principles of mathematics and economics, but also they can begin to see the close relationships between the various sectors of society.

3. The family is studied in terms of its own internal relationships and in terms of its relationships to the community. For example, the various needs of a family are considered: psychological, economic, and so forth. Considered also are the effect on the family and its members when certain needs are not met, the responsibility of the community to the family, and the problem of poverty as a breakdown in responsibility.

4. The resources of the community, food resources, industrial resources, human resources, service resources, and others, are studied in terms of the population that the area can sustain. Climate and geographical features are considered in relation to resources.

5. The customs and general culture of the people of the community are studied, permitting the introduction of the meaning of culture to people, an understanding of how cultures differ, and respect for cultures other than that of the local community.

Such examples could be multiplied, but these will indicate the essence of Makiguchi's thinking in regard to community study. All aspects of the curriculum come back to the local community as the center of the student's learning experiences. Concepts from geography, biology, botany, sociology, economics, literature, history, and other subjects become the tools for understanding and responsibly participating in the local, national, and world communities in which the student's life centers. The community itself becomes the course of study, particularly in its local manifestation for the lower grades but increasingly in its larger manifestation for the upper grades.

In this type of education there are times, Makiguchi cautioned, when the student knows more than the teacher. At such times the teacher should not try to explain but should let the new knowledge come from the students themselves. Above all the teacher should not exhibit a know-it-all attitude but should share the learning experience with the students. Sometimes, Makiguchi advised, the teacher should lead, but most of the time he should play the role of a spectator. Sometimes he should clearly point out purpose or direction, while at other times he should just be there to help. Again, the teacher should not be a boss but should leave students free to meet and solve problems. He should not be an obstacle to students who really want to learn. He should not stifle their curiosity but should help them experience the good feeling and pleasure of discovery. By these means the teacher can help students develop internal discipline, perseverance, self-respect, and self-esteem. Such goals as these can best be achieved if the teacher engages in discussion with students just as an elder brother would. In Makiguchi's view, this is the key to good teaching.

Makiguchi contrasted this style of teaching with the style of traditional education, which, he charged, did little more than fill students full of dead, useless knowledge. Such knowledge has little meaning for students; thus they lack understanding and cannot apply what they have learned to real life situations. Makiguchi was especially critical of the Japanese examination system for entrance to schools and universities. The cramming of useless, soon-to-be-forgotten information in order to pass tests was to him the height of folly and represented in acute form the deeper sickness of the whole educational system. Once this poured-in education is gone, he asked, what is left? He answered that there is nothing left: the learner is empty and is like "a person walking in the dark with a cane."[36]

Makiguchi felt strongly that Japan's educational system was extremely wasteful and uneconomical. Learning, he insisted, could not be measured in terms of the number of hours a child sat in the classroom nor by the number of teachers employed. The only valid measure of learning and teaching effectiveness must be in terms of useful and usable insights, concepts, and skills that the learners retain and that become a permanent part of their personalities. If natural education were replaced by cultural education, he predicted, children not only would learn more and retain more of what they learn, but would be able to learn it in a fraction of the time.

On the basis of this conviction, Makiguchi advocated a half-day school plan. He was convinced that a half day in school, if that half day were effectively and efficiently used to lead children in cultural educational experiences grounded in community study, was all the time needed. Furthermore, the child needs time to engage in other kinds of activity. Time spent in study needs to be balanced by time spent in physical exercise and in creative, productive work experience.

There were several implications of the half-day school proposal to which Makiguchi addressed himself. First of all, he wished to make it clear that children were not to have more time out of the classroom simply to be idle. Guidance would be required from both teachers and parents to assist children in planning fruitful, self-learning activities in which they were personally interested. As examples of the kinds of activities that children might choose to engage in, Makiguchi suggested that a child might study in the area of industrial or technological education; he might study and acquire skill in the occupation of his parents; he might engage in other kinds of work experience or on-the-job training for which he is suited; he might pursue some specialty that will be useful to him in the future; he might develop skill in one or more athletic activites in which he is interested and has capability.

A second aspect of Makiguchi's proposal for a half-day school program was its implications for the community. In effect,

Makiguchi sought to end the isolation of the school and make it an integral part of community life. This would mean, from the standpoint of the school, that the entire community would become the student's classroom. It would also mean that the members of the community would become participants in the teaching task. Makiguchi felt strongly about this. He was, for example, highly critical of the industrial education program as it then existed in Japanese schools. Industrial education courses were being taught by what he called "nonindustrial educators," teachers who had no practical experience in the job skill being taught. Consequently, students received only superficial training in the skill. In Makiguchi's plan the student would spend some time working in an on-the-job-training type of situation and would thus receive some instruction from members of the community who were actually working in the skill the student was studying. Makiguchi recognized that this would require a high degree of cooperation and teamwork from business and industrial people and from the entire community. Not only did he think this would be possible, but he believed it would enable the school and the community to develop a healthy and positive relationship with each other that would be beneficial to both.

A third aspect of Makiguchi's half-day proposal was its saving in the cost of education. School plants and facilities could be used for one group in the morning and for a second group in the afternoon; and where necessary, they could also be used in the evening for a third group of students. This emphasis on economy, it will be noted, follows quite naturally from Makiguchi's basic views and recommendations for the development of a healthy educational system. Economy in education means that there is no waste in utilizing the abilities of teachers and developing the abilities of students. The economizing of experience and time in education was in fact, according to Makiguchi, one of the principles of his theory of value. Thus his advice to teachers who wanted to assist in establishing the new pedagogy included three slogans: start with experience, make value the aim, and make economizing the principle.

This, in brief, was Makiguchi's alternative to the educational system of his day. Satoshi Ikeda holds that it is one of the tragedies of Japanese education that Makiguchi's educational proposals were ignored by the Japanese people and their government during his lifetime. He believes that Makiguchi's educational ideas may contain the solutions to many of modern Japan's educational problems. In fact, if the Japanese had listened to Makiguchi, Ikeda contends, they would not now be experiencing a serious crisis in their educational system—a crisis that has seen a major part of the nation's colleges and universities on strike and in rebellion in recent years.

How valid is this assessment of Makiguchi and his work? Are we dealing with one of the great educators of history or, as many of the educators who knew him perceived him to be, with an insignificant school teacher who had some wild ideas? Do Makiguchi's educational philosophy and pedagogy contain insights of value for modern educators? My research led me to conclude that Makiguchi does, indeed, merit recognition as one of the world's great educational thinkers and that his work does contain meaningful and valuable insights for the present day. What then are some of the factors that led to these conclusions?

An Indigenous Japanese Pragmatism

It is my view that Makiguchi stands today as the chief spokes-man for Japanese pragmatism and for the new education that he believed must be developed both in accordance with the principles of pragmatism and as its handmaiden in the pursuit of a better life for the masses of mankind. It would be correct to say, in fact, that Makiguchi's pragmatic educational philosophy is the only indigenous expression of pragmatism in Japanese culture that has endured and has contemporary significance. This assertion will require some validation and clarification because, as students of Japanese intellectual history are aware, there were attempts at the formulation of pragmatic philosophies in Japan early in the present century, and the influence of Dewey has been pronounced in Japan during certain periods. The ideas of both James and Dewey were introduced into Japan as early as 1888.* During the next thirty years enthusiasm for pragmatic ideas developed on the part of some Japanese educators and philosophers. Dewey's educational ideas were particularly popular during this period and several of his books were translated into Japanese. His *Outline of a Critical Theory of Ethics* appeared in 1900 and *School and Society* the following year. *Democracy and Education* was published in Japanese in 1918. In actual teaching situations, some educators proceeded during this period to apply both Dewey's ideas and progressive educational ideas from other sources.

Active promotion of pragmatism was short-lived, however. By 1930 both pragmatism and progressive educational practice had ceased to be significant in Japanese education. Various explanations have been offered for the decline of pragmatism in Japan, including that of the nationalists to the effect that pragmatism did not suit the Japanese mentality. A more realistic assessment is that of Kobayashi: "The interests in philosophy of Americans and Japanese had similar histories until about the

---

*For a discussion of pragmatism in Japan during this early period, see Gino K. Piovesana, *Recent Japanese Philosophical Thought, 1862–1962* (Tokyo: Enderle Bookstore, 1963), pp. 62–73.

turn of the century. Both groups had studied J. S. Mill and Spencer and the Kantians with great intensity. However, when American philosophy began to come of age with the appearance of William James and Dewey, the dominance of German philosophy continued in Japan, partly because of the stimulation of close cultural ties with Germany, which were encouraged by the government. The interest was further perpetuated by the predominance of philosophy professors who specialized in German philosophy; it was reinforced by the deterioration of relations with England and America, as Japan joined Germany in its tide of fascism. These factors were also in operation in the area of pedagogy and educational philosophy."[37]

Dewey's educational ideas declined in popularity during the years prior to World War II; however, even during the heyday of his influence in Japan, that is to say, immediately following World War I, his views were not grasped by the Japanese as a complete philosophy of education. This was true not only in Japan; Americans, too, largely failed to understand the deeper implications of what Dewey was saying. Judith Groch, for example, writes that the "spirit behind Dewey's words was ignored, and his words, notably ambiguous, were misunderstood. Watson, who had been Dewey's pupil and who had been influenced by Dewey's pragmatic philosophy, remarked years later that he had never really understood what Dewey was talking about. Apparently Watson was not alone. Mediocre teachers milked the doctrine for its more attractive concepts. 'Learning by doing' and 'freedom of expression' became ends in themselves, and the 'object lesson' was vested with magical properties and sprinkled throughout the curriculum even when glowingly inappropriate. Dewey, with good reason, distrusted teachers and textbooks, preferring experiment and the laboratory as a means of discovery. But Dewey never intended the laboratory experiment to be a cheap, mechanical imitation of science in which the student knew ahead of time what he was supposed to find."[38]

In Japan too Dewey's ideas about teaching methods were most emphasized and moved most educational reformers. The important thing to note here, however, is that in the midst of a general decline of interest in both Dewey and pragmatism in Japan prior to World War II, Makiguchi continued to preach his own pragmatic philosophy. While in the end it was on religious grounds that he was imprisoned, his continued espousal of pragmatic educational views that were considered Western and therefore foreign and dangerous, as well as disputes over religious ritual, led to attitudes of hostility and suspicion toward him on the part of Japanese educators and government officials.

Study of developments and trends in Japanese education in the post–World War II period points up the need within Japanese society for an integrative educational philosophy and pedagogy such as that developed by Makiguchi. Following Japan's defeat in 1945, officers of the Allied occupation effected what has often been referred to as a "bloodless revolution" in Japanese education. Yasumasa Oshima states that in the course of just a few weeks a complete reversal of educational policy occurred, from a situation in which education was completely controlled by the government for its own purposes to one in which education was completely freed from central governmental control.[39] The new situation was interpreted by liberal and progressively inclined educators, whose voices had been muted since the ascendancy of the Japanese military in the early 1930s, as an invitation to participate actively in shaping the "new Japanese education." Although a sharp reactionary movement that developed in Japanese society following the return of sovereignty to Japan in the early 1950s resulted in the loss of many of the educational reforms of the occupation

period, liberal and progressive educators have continued to
exert a significant influence in Japanese education.

The influence of the occupation on Japanese education was
predominantly an American influence. Ronald S. Anderson,
who was a member of the American military government's
educational staff, indicates in his report, "Japan: Three Epochs
of Modern Education," that occupation authorities sought to
replace the authoritarian, centralized educational system,
which had been developed by the Japanese government, with
the best in American educational philosophy and practice.[40]
Emphasis was upon the individual.

One Japanese educator whom Anderson interviewed in 1957
observed that "the prewar education of Japan taught patriotism and reverence for the Emperor, but failed to develop
personality or teach citizenship. The new education neglects
patriotism to some extent, but does develop personality and
teach responsible citizenship. The Fundamental Law of Education which expresses the policy of the new education is
an accurate statement of the ideals of the new Japan. The
conservatives say it is not congenial to Japanese historical
experience or tradition, but the young people really *have* experienced the values of the Fundamental Law of Education.
Young women, especially, have been emancipated. Japan went
through a bloodless revolution during the Occupation, and
the new value system coincides with the new statement of
principles. . . . The old people regard the defeat and the
Occupation as an extremely miserable experience, but some
of the young people look on it as necessary to have accomplished the revolutionary emancipation."[41]

This statement vividly portrays one of the most striking characteristics of Japanese society and Japanese education during
the decades following the termination of the occupation; namely, the constant tug-of-war that has occurred between the

conservatives and those of a more liberal or progressive bent who have been nurtured and challenged by the democratic stream of philosophical thought in Japanese educational history, which the occupation reinforced.

It is my assessment that these polar tendencies in Japanese society and education, and the struggle that has issued from their confrontation, have had a healthy and largely beneficial effect on the society and on the educational system. It is very possible, in fact, that the strength and vitality of the Japanese economy has been due in some measure to the interplay of these opposing forces. However, the observation may also be made that this struggle has consumed a major part of the creative energy of educators in Japan during this period. As a result of this preoccupation with the conservative-liberal struggle, educators have not devoted sufficient attention to the development of an indigenous, forward-looking educational philosophy and pedagogy capable of meeting the needs of the Japanese people in the years ahead. It is my belief that Makiguchi's theory of value and his value-creating pedagogy is such an indigenous philosophy and pedagogy. While his philosophy and pedagogy developed on foundations provided for the most part by John Dewey and Lester Ward, they represent a unique and creative formulation of a pragmatic educational position within Japan, and one that can enable the Japanese to share in the task of bringing a more humane society into being.

In Retrospect

One must recognize that, when one looks closely at Makiguchi's proposals for the transformation of Japanese education and society, there are some areas in which he is vulnerable to criticism. For example, he was vehement in his denunciation of "abstract philosophers," or "theorists" as he called them, and called for a completely inductive approach to the development of a practical pedagogy for teachers. Yet he proceeded to develop an equally philosophical, or theoretical, position and insisted that his proposed pedagogy could not be understood even in the slightest degree without first understanding the philosophical position that he had outlined. At this point Makiguchi's biases and resentments at his exclusion from the academic and intellectual circles of his society seem to have influenced his thinking.

Another limiting factor that may be pointed to in regard to Makiguchi's proposals for educational reform is that they were for the most part speculative and untested despite his emphasis on scientific method and experimentation. The only experimenting ever done using the teaching methods and approaches that he advocated was the little he did within the Tokyo public school system. This was necessarily limited because of the realities of that system and the indifference of officials to the kinds of reforms that Makiguchi advocated.

Josei Toda utilized some of Makiguchi's methods in a private tutoring school that he established in 1923 to prepare primary school students for the middle-school entrance examination. Toda's experimentation seems to have made a firm believer out of him. In fact, he became quite wealthy as a result of the sale of books that he published to assist students who were preparing for these examinations.[42] Toda's work, however, could hardly be considered an adequate test of Makiguchi's methods. Furthermore, the use of value-creating pedagogical methods to aid students in preparing for entrance examinations would appear not only to be in direct conflict with Makiguchi's major criticisms of Japanese education but also to have the effect of supporting and strengthening the system rather than reforming it.

It should also be acknowledged that there is no mistaking the philosophical naiveté in Makiguchi's writings. The fact that he was a self-taught philosopher will be detected very quickly by the competent scholar. It should be understood that my comparison of Makiguchi with Dewey in terms of the type of role each played in the intellectual history of his respective country does not imply that Makiguchi's grasp of the field of philosophy was as extensive as Dewey's nor that his stature as a philosopher compares with that of Dewey. Dewey had access to the entire range of Western philosophical thought. He had opportunity to study and teach at the leading institutions of higher learning that his culture possessed. During the course of his teaching career he had opportunity to confront and be challenged by scores of razor-sharp minds in the fields of philosophy, education, psychology, and sociology. Moreover, Dewey rode the crest of one of the central tendencies and moods of his time.

Makiguchi, in contrast, had but limited access to the literature of the Western philosophical tradition. His reading was necessarily limited to translations, which were often of questionable quality.[43] Makiguchi had no college or university training, and with few exceptions he was denied access to the resources of the university community. While he read widely and brought the ideas of many brilliant minds into his work, he was frequently beyond his depth and unable to grasp or at least to express the larger implications of the ideas about which he wrote. It was at this point that the works of Dewey and Ward were very important to Makiguchi. Both the writings of Dewey as an educator and those of Ward as a sociologist provided the initial core of Makiguchi's own thinking, thus enabling him to evaluate and interpret the widely differing ideas and philosophical positions to which his reading had exposed him.

In view of Makiguchi's limitations and handicaps, however, the quality of his insights and the extent to which he anticipated the problems and needs of the individual in a mass society are nothing short of remarkable. Thus, while such criticisms as those noted above are valid and should be taken into account, they do not diminish the importance of Makiguchi's work as a significant contribution to educational thought.

Recent developments in the field of education tend to confirm many of the reforms that Makiguchi advocated. Van Cleve Morris, in a review of Charles Silberman's recent book *Crisis in the Classroom: The Remaking of American Education*, comments: "As the professional educator reads Silberman, there is a haunting, back-of-the-cerebrum sense of having heard it all before. But where? Silberman himself provides a clue to the answer. Informal schooling and experience centered education, he implies, are John Dewey reissued. Silberman's *Crisis* is the kind of book which needs writing every few years to remind us that, half a century later, we still have not carried into practice the sound and sensible theories of this 20th-century pedagogical architect."[44]

Much the same thing that Morris says of Dewey's work could be said with reference to Makiguchi's. There are some areas in which Makiguchi may legitimately be said to have added worthwhile insights to Dewey's work. Makiguchi's concepts of value and value creation and his emphasis on community study and the social responsibility of individuals as creators of value would seem to be of this nature. In most respects, however, one finds little in Makiguchi that cannot also be found in Dewey. The value of Makiguchi's work, then, does not lie in its being greatly different from that of Dewey. Rather, its strength lies in the fact that it provides support and confirmation from yet another culture for the efficacy of education based on an open, experiential model in contrast to the transmission-of-knowledge model that we have inherited from the medieval period of western-European history.

4 Makiguchi and the Soka Gakkai Movement

Educational Reformer Before World War II

Tsunesaburo Makiguchi, as previous chapters have shown, was a reformer. Like Johann Pestalozzi a century earlier, his life centered on one consuming purpose, the elevating and enhancing of the life of his fellows. Like Pestalozzi, too, Makiguchi was often misunderstood and rejected by the people he sought to help and was mistrusted by the government to which he professed allegiance. During the greater part of his life he sought to achieve his objectives by working as a teacher and administrator in the educational structures of Japanese society. A reconstruction of the events and relationships of the last fifteen years of his life suggests, however, that a major shift occurred in his thinking with respect to the means by which people dedicated to reform could best pursue their objectives. Essentially this was a shift from educational to religious means of effecting reform. The broad outline of the conditions and incidents involved in this shift in Makiguchi's position was traced in chapter two. We should now look more closely at the shift itself and some of the factors involved in it.

It may be observed, first of all, that up to the present time no specific statement has come to light in which Makiguchi recognized and acknowledged this shift in his thought and outlook. Thus it can only be deduced from an examination of his writings, the record of his activities during this period, and from reports of people who were acquainted with him at this time. A second observation that may be made is that this shift occurred gradually over a period of nearly a decade.

In tracing the developments of this period, three factors emerge that may explain this shift in Makiguchi's outlook and approach to reform. One is the series of personal tragedies and hardships that he experienced during the twenties and early thirties, including the deaths of four of his children. Even more important may have been the cultural and political environment in which he pursued his educational career. To put it bluntly, Makiguchi, after devoting nearly forty years of his life to trying to bring about change in Japan's personality-stifling, tradition-bound system of education, had to face the hard reality that he had failed. His efforts to humanize the educational system and increase its effectiveness had been thwarted at every turn by both the rigidity of the culture and the increasing dominance of the military in national life.

A reasonable evaluation of the data may be that it was primarily a sense of frustration and futility, which accompanied this recognition of his powerlessness to bring about change in Japanese society through educational means, that led him eventually to see religion rather than education as the most strategic means for effecting societal change. This analysis was borne out in interviews with the remaining members of the small cadre of young men who gathered around Makiguchi during the 1930s, as well as with less intimate participants in the movement that he initiated. It is the general assessment of these people that what Makiguchi and they initially attempted was an educational revolution and that the emphasis turned increasingly to a religious one immediately prior to and during World War II. Representative of the people whose observations supported this general conclusion were a Nichiren Shoshu priest, who was still active in the sect, and a school teacher who had severed ties with Makiguchi's movement in the late 1930s because, in his view, its orientation had already become too religious.

A third factor in the shift from an educational to a religious orientation was Makiguchi's conversion to Nichiren Shoshu in 1928. In fact, Murata writes that Soka Gakkai would not exist today had it not been for a seemingly minor incident in 1928, when Makiguchi was principal of Shirogane Primary School in Tokyo. A Nichiren Shoshu adherent who was a reporter for a trade paper visited Makiguchi's school. The reporter subsequently introduced Makiguchi to Sokei Mitani, an influential Nichiren Shoshu believer and the principal of a Tokyo business high school. It was through association with Mitani that Makiguchi was converted to faith in Nichren Shoshu.[1]

As far as can be determined this was Makiguchi's first serious interest in religion. Murata's research reveals that Makiguchi's family religion in Niigata was Nichiren Shu, a related but dif-

ferent sect from Nichiren Shoshu. He had also been mildly interested at times in Christianity. In fact, he had been quite deeply
influenced in the development of his educational philosophy
and practices by such Christian educators as Inazo Nitobe and
Kanzo Uchimura and cited Uchimura's work, *Chijinron*
(Theory of Land and People), as making a significant contribution to his own work *Jinsei Chirigaku*.[2] However, in neither
his attachment to his family religion nor his interest in Christianity is there evidence of serious concern with or attention to
religious matters as such.[3] Furthermore, even after his conversion to Nichiren Shoshu, it appears that Makiguchi's religious convictions matured slowly, very probably growing in
intensity as his faith in educational reform diminished.

At this point one must acknowledge a paradox in Makiguchi's
philosophical orientation. His educational work and the writings that grew out of that work reveal him as a thoroughgoing
pragmatist. In volume one of *Soka Kyoikugaku Taikei,* for
example, he wrote that any argument that is not scientific or
cannot be proved experimentally will only result in endless
dispute. Even though what science has been able to explain
thus far is limited, human beings have to solve actual problems
that they face in daily living. It is unfruitful, therefore, to
waste time in metaphysical consideration.[4] In contrast with
this position are statements in *The Philosophy of Value* (Kachiron),
the reissue of volume two of *Soka Kyoikugaku Taikei* edited and
supplemented by Josei Toda after Makiguchi's death, that
seem to constitute a direct refutation of Makiguchi's relativistic, pragmatic philosophy, advocating instead an unquestioning
faith in an Object of Worship.[5]

Brannen was one of the first scholars to note this apparent
discrepancy in Makiguchi's work and thought. It was his conclusion that in editing *The Philosophy of Value* Toda, the second
president of Soka Gakkai, "took the liberty of bringing what

may have been originally a purely utilitarian philosophical treatise into conformity with the teachings of the Nichiren Sho Sect [Nichiren Shoshu]."[6] My research verifies Brannen's conclusion. An example cited as evidence of such editing liberties on Toda's part is a reference to atomic bombs, which Makiguchi could not have known about.[7] This evidence led me to conjecture that Makiguchi maintained his pragmatic position to the end and that it was later leaders who turned the movement to its postwar emphasis on the mystical and metaphysical. This turned out not to be the case.

Thus, while there is no doubt that Toda did make changes in *The Philosophy of Value,* as Brannen points out, it is very likely that he did so fully believing that Makiguchi would have made the same changes and additions had he lived. However, I have been able to find nothing in Makiguchi's original writings summarizing the results of forty years in education that is contradictory to a pragmatic position. If further research bears this out, it will suggest that, although Makiguchi was converted to Nichiren Shoshu in 1928, there appears to be no evidence that Nichiren Shoshu doctrine influenced the editing of his major educational work, *Soka Kyoikugaku Taikei,* during the years 1929 to 1933.

One could argue that, since *Soka Kyoikugaku Taikei* was compiled from notes and jottings accumulated during the course of several decades, the utilitarian philosophy expressed therein represents an earlier period in Makiguchi's intellectual development and does not necessarily reflect his views during the 1930s. However, other of Makiguchi's writings of this period refute any such conclusion. *Kankyo* (Environment), a magazine for teachers published with the help of Toda and several other supporters who had organized themselves as a study society, is a case in point. Organized for the purpose of furthering Makiguchi's brand of educational reform, the group called itself

Soka Kyoiku Gakkai (Value-Creating Education Society). Soka Gakkai (Value-Creating Society), the organization that Makiguchi's followers reconstructed after World War II, now regards the formation of this study group in 1930 as its beginning. The formal organization of Soka Kyoiku Gakkai with Makiguchi as its president did not occur until 1937.[8]

Included in the ninth issue of *Kankyo*, dated November 20, 1930, is an editorial statement outlining the purpose of the publication: "The study of teaching materials and methods is something that practical educators must not neglect or take lightly; rather these matters should be the central concern of their daily living. Such study is the practical educator's source of power. Lacking such study he is just like a steam engine without fuel. . . .

"However, the average educator is too busy with his daily round of teaching activities to discover and collect life-related teaching material. It is hoped that this magazine can become a companion, or partner, to the classroom teacher by carrying a share of the burden of his school work. Thus teachers who wish to be on the front line of educational practice will not have to worry about collecting materials and will be able to devote their full attention to the teaching task itself.

"Scientific pedagogy, or systematic research in teaching methods, and collecting living teaching material are vital aspects of the teaching task. The relationship of these two aspects of education to education as a whole is just like the relationship between a cart and its wheels or a bird and its wings.

"In this issue of *Kankyo* we are giving special attention to Mr. Makiguchi's book *Soka Kyoikugaku Taikei* because we believe it can be a great help to the busy teacher. At the present time, when education is stalemated and deadlocked, Mr. Makiguchi's pedagogy is truly like a beacon lighting the way to a rebirth in education."

The articles in this issue bear out the sentiment and intent of this editorial. In a major article, entitled "The Essential Elements of Value-Creating Pedagogy," Makiguchi, after critically examining Japanese education and society, wrote that education is the key element in any move toward the revolutionary reconstruction of society. Not just any kind of education will do; value-creating pedagogy is the first step toward bringing about urgently needed changes in human attitudes, in educational institutions, and in the social structures of Japanese society.

In Makiguchi's view, among the factors working against the development of an effective educational system based on value-creating pedagogy was the government's stranglehold on education as a result of its operation and control of teacher-training institutions. The government had done nothing, he charged, to encourage creative teaching or to improve the status of teachers and attract and hold competent people in the teaching ranks. What Japan desperately needed, he wrote, was an educational-research center where educational problems could be scientifically studied and educational experimentation carried on. The school, Makiguchi insisted, must become society's laboratory. As such, it would function as a bridge between the individual and his family and the society at large. In order for the nation to make orderly development and progress, then, value-creating pedagogy must be studied and understood not only by educators but by politicians, as well.

Included also in this ninth issue of *Kankyo* were two articles by leading progressive educators and statesmen supporting Makiguchi and his efforts to promote educational and social reform. One article was written by Inazo Nitobe. The other was a brief statement signed by twenty-eight prominent individuals, including Tsuyoshi Inukai, who later was prime minister from December 1931 to May 1932. That Makiguchi had support from people of this stature suggests the possibility that recognition of Makiguchi as an educator would very likely have increased in marked degree if the political climate in Japan had moved toward openness and democratic participation during the 1930s. However, as history records, this did not occur. In May, 1932, Prime Minister Inukai was assassinated. From that point on the position of progressively oriented educators and statesmen deteriorated rapidly. With this development, Makiguchi's last hope for achieving reform through purely educational means began to diminish.

The study group continued and its membership increased, primarily through the addition of teachers who had become frustrated in their teaching efforts or had been "blackballed" by the government for leftist leanings or activities. But as the 1930s wore on and as the military regime tightened its hold over the various sectors of society, the channels through which Makiguchi could influence teachers and educators became closed to him. In my view, as this occurred there began to dawn in Makiguchi's mind the possibilities afforded by Nichiren Shoshu for achievement of reform objectives. One indication that a shift did occur in Makiguchi's thinking, from educational to religious means of achieving reform, is a small publication written by Makiguchi and printed in 1937. This pamphlet, bearing the title *Soka Kyoikuho no Kagakuteki Choshukyoteki Jikken Shomei* (Practical Experimentation in Value-Creating Educational Methods Through Science and Supreme Religion), contrasts sharply with his writings of the early 1930s. Thus whereas *Kankyo,* for example, was concerned exclusively with the educational dimensions and implications of value-creating pedagogy, the 1937 publication is preoccupied with religious concerns and exhortations.

At this time, too, Makiguchi apparently began to give more attention to the possibilities in organized or corporate action and power. Early in 1937 sixty people who had become interested in and responsive to Makiguchi's ideas met at the Kikusuitei, a Tokyo restaurant, and formally organized Soka Kyoiku Gakkai. This was considered the first general meeting or conference of the organization. A second such meeting was not held until three years later, when membership is said to have increased to three or four hundred people. From this time until the disbanding of the organization by the government in 1943, the members met semiannually to report on the results of their educational research programs and on their personal experiences.

Following the 1937 meeting the membership of Soka Kyoiku Gakkai began to change. Whereas prior to this time the people associated with Makiguchi were primarily teachers interested in some aspect of education—reform, research, or Makiguchi's educational insights—people from other stations and walks of life now began to come into the organization, drawn by the religious elements of Nichiren Shoshu as these were interpreted by Makiguchi. That such a change in the composition of the organization's membership actually occurred is suggested by items in *Kachi Sozo* (The Creation of Value), a monthly periodical that the organization began publishing in 1941. Interspersed in this periodical, along with feature articles about value-creating pedagogy, are the testimonials of people who claimed to have found various benefits and blessings as the result of adhering to Nichiren Shoshu religious practice, or of membership in Soka Kyoiku Gakkai, or of following the guidance of President Makiguchi. For example, in the first issue of *Kachi Sozo* is the group testimonial of twenty-seven mothers that as a result of joining Soka Kyoiku Gakkai they had experienced painless childbirth. Another feature of *Kachi Sozo* was an admonition to members to participate in *shakubuku* activities, a militant and forceful method of converting people.

The feature articles also suggest Nichiren Shoshu influence. These articles contrast markedly with those of *Kankyo* and *Soka Kyoikugaku Taikei* of a decade earlier.

As the shift from chiefly educational concerns to a combined emphasis on education and the Buddhism of Nichiren Shoshu occurred, the original members tended to respond in one of two ways. The response of some of them was simply to drop out of the organization. It is difficult to estimate the number who actually responded in this way. I interviewed an elementary school principal who indicated that he had left Makiguchi's movement because of the shift to religious concerns. It was his opinion that others had left for the same reason, but he was unable to cite specific cases. Other members, probably the majority of Makiguchi's original disciples, continued in the organization and shared in the attempt to integrate Makiguchi's educational philosophy and pedagogy with Nichiren Shoshu Buddhism.

Apparently the Japanese government did not approve of the type of material printed in *Kachi Sozo,* for publication was suspended after the ninth issue by government order. However, a printed report, *Taizen Seikatsu Jisshoroku* (Witness to Abundant Life), of the fifth conference of Soka Kyoiku Gakkai, in 1942, contains the same kinds of articles and testimonials. The following year, on July 6, 1943, Makiguchi, Toda, and nineteen other people—the entire upper-echelon leadership of the organization—were arrested and jailed for their intransigent opposition to government-supported State Shinto.* On November 18, 1944, at the age of seventy-three, Makiguchi died of malnutrition at Sugamo Prison. The only record available, to my knowledge, concerning Makiguchi's intellectual and emotional life during his seventeen-month imprisonment is a series of post-card messages that he wrote to his daughter-in-

*For further details of the arrests, see Murata, *Japan's New Buddhism* (New York & Tokyo: Walker/Weatherhill, 1969), pp. 83–84.

law, Sadako. Study of these messages suggests that Makiguchi remained firm in his loyalty and dedication to Nichiren Shoshu to the end.

Postwar Reconstruction

Although Makiguchi's leadership of the movement that he had initiated ended with his death in prison in 1944, his importance did not diminish. Through the lives of those who had been closely associated with him, his influence continued to be felt during the reconstruction of the movement after the war. Chief among these associates was Josei Toda, who, as a young school teacher, had met Makiguchi in 1920. Toda joined Nichiren Shoshu in 1928 along with Makiguchi. However, it appears that prior to his arrest in 1943 business was of far more interest to Toda than was religion. During the early and mid-1920s he had experienced dire poverty, which was undoubtedly a contributing factor to a series of tragedies in his life, including the death of an infant daughter, the loss of his wife from tuberculosis, and the contraction of the same disease himself. His fortunes began to improve, however, with the publication of some books to help students preparing for middle-school entrance examinations. One of these, a book on arithmetic, was extremely successful, selling more than a million copies. This was the beginning of Toda's business activities. By the time of his arrest in the summer of 1943 he controlled seventeen companies, with two more about to be added to his business holdings. His fortune is said to have amounted at that time to more than ¥6,000,000 or, at the prewar exchange rate, about $1,500,000.[9]

The ordeal in prison brought to Toda a more intense re-

ligious experience. Interested as he was in the study of science
and mathematics, Toda found it difficult to believe in anything
that was not logically convincing. But as he read the *Hoke-kyo*,
or Lotus Sutra (the Buddhist scripture that Nichiren Shoshu
includes in its teachings), and the sacred writings of Nichiren,
and particularly as he chanted the *daimoku* (the sacred phrase
Nam-myoho-renge-kyo, literally, "Devotion to the Wonderful
Law Lotus Sutra"), a profound change came over him and he
became convinced that at last he had found the true meaning
of life. This experience, together with shock and grief at the
news of Makiguchi's death, led Toda to vow that he would
devote the rest of his life to spreading the teachings of Nichiren.[10]

After his release from prison on July 3, 1945, Toda set about
the twofold task of rebuilding his business empire, which had
been completely destroyed, and gathering together the frag-
ments of Soka Kyoiku Gakkai. Successive business ventures
ended in failure, due probably not so much to lack of ability
on Toda's part as to the unstable economic conditions of the
postwar period. His final venture, a credit cooperative, col-
lapsed in 1950. While the rebuilding of Soka Kyoiku Gakkai
eventually proved more successful, its chances appeared bleak
at the end of the war. All the leaders of the organization, with
the exception of Makiguchi, Toda, and Shuhei Yajima, had
broken under government pressure and had renounced both
their faith and their allegiance to the organization. (Although
Murata indicates that only Toda stood with Makiguchi in
his refusal to be broken by the government,[11] Satoshi Ikeda
writes that Yajima also stood firm.[12]) Moreover, the rank-and-
file members were scattered and there was no way of regaining
contact with them.

Against this background Toda launched into the task of re-
constructing Soka Kyoiku Gakkai. (The word kyoiku was later
dropped from the name of the reconstructed organization.)

He was convinced that the organization had disintegrated because its members had been weak in doctrinal discipline. He determined, therefore, that in the new organization greater emphasis would be placed on inculcating the teachings of both the Lotus Sutra and Nichiren upon the members. Toward this end he opened a seminar on the Lotus Sutra at Daiseki-ji on January 1, 1946, with three followers in attendance. Thereafter he lectured three times a week at his office in downtown Tokyo; and as its membership increased, the second floor of his office eventually developed into the headquarters of the organization.

In a meeting of leaders held on May 1, 1946, Toda was named chairman of the board of directors, the same position he had held in the prewar organization. However, he resisted moves to make him president. Not until the collapse of his business ventures in 1950 did he consent to assume the position of president, which had been left open since Makiguchi's death. At the time Toda assumed the presidency he reasoned that his business failures were divine punishment for his failure to devote his full energy to the rebuilding of Soka Gakkai.[13] Up to that time the growth of the organization had been modest at best. Furthermore, with the collapse of Toda's business ventures many of his followers, including some Soka Gakkai leaders, left the organization. Toda himself was apparently discouraged occasionally. In March, 1951, he is reported to have remarked sarcastically: "At this rate [ninety-five families per month] we can reach an enormous number in ten thousand years."[14] Yet when he was inaugurated as president at the general meeting of Soka Gakkai in Tokyo on May 3, 1951, Toda vowed to "convert 750,000 families before I die. If this is not achieved by the time of my death, don't hold a funeral service for me but throw my ashes into the sea off Shinagawa."[15] While this goal was at the time dismissed by some observers as the prediction of an idle dreamer, prior to his death in 1958 the membership of Soka Gakkai did in fact reach the figure that had been set by Toda.

Although a detailed discussion of Nichiren Shoshu and its belief system is beyond the scope of this book, an understanding of certain basic features of Nichiren Shoshu is essential in order to place the developments of the decade following Toda's assumption of the presidency in proper perspective. The unique relationship that presently exists between Nichiren Shoshu and Soka Gakkai as a lay organization of the sect had its beginnings during the early postwar period. While some of the frictions that had marred relationships between the Nichiren Shoshu leadership and the leadership of the lay movement prior to Makiguchi's death continued into the postwar period, these frictions had been satisfactorily resolved by the time of Toda's death on April 2, 1958.[16]

The goal that believers in Nichiren Shoshu seek to attain is *kosen rufu* (literally, "the spreading of Buddhism through the whole world"). Buddhism in this context means Nichiren Shoshu Buddhism, which for believers is the only true Buddhism. This uncompromising belief in Nichiren Shoshu Buddhism as the only true faith is based on a unique interpretation of the Lotus Sutra and the life of Nichiren, a thirteenth-century Japanese Buddhist priest.* Briefly, according to Nichiren Shoshu, Nichiren is the fulfillment of Buddhist teachings in the present day. He is hailed as the original, eternal Buddha, meriting from contemporary Buddhists even greater reverence and respect than Sakyamuni, the historical Buddha and the chief Buddha of the Lotus Sutra.†

Murata gives the following historical background of the de-

---

*For an account of the life and teachings of Nichiren, see Masaharu Anesaki, *Nichiren, the Buddhist Prophet* (Cambridge: Harvard University Press, 1949).

†For further information on Nichiren Shoshu doctrine, see *The Nichiren Shoshu Sokagakkai* (Tokyo: Seikyo Press, 1966).

velopment of Nichiren Shoshu: "Shortly after Nichiren's death, one of his chief disciples, Nikko, broke with the other five and left the temple of Kuon-ji at Minobu, Nichiren's last base for evangelical activities. While the other disciples formed the Nichiren Shu (Nichiren sect), with Kuon-ji as head temple, Nikko formed a sect of his own based on a different interpretation of his mentor's teaching from that of the other disciples. One of the branches of this sect later came to be known as Nichiren Shoshu [literally, "the orthodox sect of Nichiren"], whose head temple is Taiseki-ji [*sic*] at Fujinomiya, near Mount Fuji.

"The two sects remain rivals to this day, but it is only recently that Nichiren Shoshu has won more adherents than Nichiren Shu, thanks largely to Soka Gakkai's conversion activities."[17]

Nichiren, particularly during the latter part of his life, was militant in his insistence that his interpretation of Buddhism and the Lotus Sutra was the only true belief. All other religions, he insisted, were false, corrupt, and evil and consequently must be destroyed. When the government officials of his day disregarded his preachments, Nichiren predicted that dire consequences would befall the country. Some of these predictions materialized, thus strengthening Nichiren's credibility.

Historically there are within Buddhist teachings two principal methods of propagating the faith. These are *shoju* and *shakubuku*. Murata writes that "Soka Gakkai's intensive conversion method, *shakubuku*, has become identified in the public mind with Soka Gakkai itself. *Shakubuku*, however, is neither an invention nor a monopoly of Soka Gakkai or even Nichiren Shoshu. It is one of the two traditional Buddhist methods of conversion, the other being *shoju*. Buddhist sutras refer to them both, as did Nichiren in his writings. *Shakubuku*, literally meaning 'break and subdue,' is the forceful method of conversion, while *shoju* is the moderate, conciliatory approach."[18] Understanding this element of Nichiren Shoshu belief throws some light on Makiguchi's behavior during the last two or three years of his life prior to his arrest in 1943. It is not hard to imagine that Makiguchi, observing his own failure to further educational reform, might have found it easy to identify with Nichiren and accept the principle of shakubuku as a means of achieving his goals. This, at any rate, seems a possible explanation of activities that he engaged in during the years immediately prior to his arrest.

Soka Gakkai recognizes and employs both shoju and shakubuku in its proselytizing activities. It was shakubuku, however, that Toda made the keystone of his efforts to develop Soka Gakkai after he became president in 1951, on the grounds that, just as in Nichiren's day, Japan at that time was full of evil religions and their adherents. In his inaugural address Toda told his followers that the goal of kosen rufu could be attained only when "all of you take on evil religions and convert everyone in the country."[19] Toda's followers took his counsel seriously, and shakubuku came to be central to the meaning of membership in Soka Gakkai. The result of this development is a matter of record.

When Toda assumed the presidency, Soka Gakkai was just one among many new religious movements that had mushroomed after World War II. H. Neill McFarland aptly describes this period as the "rush hour of the gods." In his book bearing this title he writes: "Prior to 1945, the Japanese people suffered through a long period of totalitarianism, during which religious bodies were either suppressed or regimented as thought-control agencies. Hence, at the end of the war, when complete freedom of religion was guaranteed as one of the cardinal principles in Japan's new day, the way was open for innumerable captive and incipient religious movements to become independent sects and for new 'prophets' to let their voices be heard."[20] In 1951 few Japanese had ever heard of

Soka Gakkai; by the end of the decade the reverse was true. In 1960 it was difficult to find a Japanese who had not formed some opinion about Soka Gakkai. From a membership of some 500 families in 1951, the organization had, by the end of the decade, not only grown to but surpassed Toda's goal of 750,000 families.

The tactical method that made this possible was shakubuku. But what was behind the method? What was the driving force in the development of Soka Gakkai? An analysis of Soka Gakkai literature reveals two major and intimately interrelated appeals that attract and hold members to the movement. These two appeals are expressed in the literature as a twofold objective: "to save the whole world through the attainment of each individual's happiness in life." As we shall see later, both the individual and the collective appeal are important factors in the growth and staying power of Soka Gakkai. During the 1950s, however, the individual appeal was particularly emphasized. Murata notes that Toda frequently reminded his followers of earthly benefits they would receive from conducting shakubuku. On August 3, 1951, he told an audience: "You carry on *shakubuku* with conviction. If you don't do it now, let me tell you, you will never become happy."[21] On September 1, 1954, he gave the following explanation to members: "Let me tell you why you must conduct *shakubuku*. This is not to make Soka Gakkai larger but for you to become happier. . . . There are many people in the world who are suffering from poverty and disease. The only way to make them really happy is to *shakubuku* them. You might say it is sufficient for you to pray at home, but unless you carry out *shakubuku* you will not receive any divine benefit. A believer who has forgotten to *shakubuku* will receive no such benefit."[22]

Kazuo Kasahara gives further evidence of the strength of Soka Gakkai's appeal to the desire for individual benefit. The Japanese people during the immediate postwar period, he points out, particularly those with limited usable skills and little education, felt overpowered by the "hardships arising from poverty, illness, and dissension. . . . They continued to exert themselves to the utmost to improve their lot, but there was a limit to what they could do. . . . Some of them began to turn for help to new religions rather than the established ones. They felt that they had already come to the end of their tether and could no longer stand their misery. . . . Many people in postwar Japan jumped at religion in expectation of tangible rewards as the immediate result of their belief and prayers. They wished to be freed from poverty, illness, and trouble the moment they embraced the faith."[23]

Kasahara goes on to point out that many new religious groups sprang up at this time to take advantage of the situation of the masses. It was not long, however, until people began to realize that they had been cheated by the new religions and their promises of impossible gains. While Soka Gakkai was one of these new religions, it also differed in significant ways. It too promised instantaneous rewards in this world but at the same time made the promises conditional on a person's taking responsibility for making his own way in life. Perhaps the most significant thing about Soka Gakkai was that it built up and strengthened its members' confidence in their own ability to live in the world, and to live within a general frame of reference that gave meaning to each person's life.[24]

The determining factor in realizing these promises of economic success, health, and family harmony was, as indicated, the member's faithfulness in performing shakubuku. There are other incentives within the system also. For successes in shakubuku activity one is rewarded with such titles and positions as head of troops, districts, and so forth. In this connection James Dator notes that while "Soka Gakkai stresses equality of all members in that all are equal when they enter Soka Gakkai, and social position is said to make no difference within the Soka Gakkai (thus, we have been told, the janitor of a bank may be a teacher and the bank president his pupil), the Soka Gakkai provides for intraorganizational ranking on the basis of individual effort. For example, it provides persons with such culturally honored titles as 'Assistant Professor' or 'Professor' or the like on the basis of objective tests covering the doctrine and practices of Nichiren Shoshu. Thus persons who did not have an opportunity to receive higher education (and such is the case for most Soka Gakkai members) are able to be 'professors' within the Soka Gakkai."[25] Brannen stresses the new sense of identity that Soka Gakkai makes possible for people without identity: "There is a sense in which the millions of converts to Soka Gakkai are a new race, sought out and 'reclaimed.' "[26]

Apart from the incentives of tangible rewards, the member became convinced that in propagating his faith he was assisting to bring salvation, not only to himself and to the immediate object of his shakubuku efforts, but to the world, as well. This dimension of Soka Gakkai may be a significant factor in accounting for the staying power and continued growth of the movement into the present. Soka Gakkai offers the convert the opportunity not only to benefit himself, but to feel a part of a great and magnificent destiny that he, through individually creating value, can help to work out. Under such circumstances a Soka Gakkai member in the act of shakubuku could approach other people with complete sincerity and conviction. With members thus impelled and motivated, it was probably inevitable that some would go to extremes. In some cases overzealous members went so far as to use force and violence in their attempts to pressure potential converts into acquiescence.

It has been these extreme forms of shakubuku, in addition to a general suspicion of Soka Gakkai's phenomenal success itself, that have led to negative reactions from the press and the public. For example, Goichiro Fujii, director of the Public

Security Investigation Agency of the Ministry of Justice, was quoted in a major Japanese newspaper, on November 26, 1955, as saying that Soka Gakkai was "conducting a membership drive in a semigangster manner, using a military organization." Although Mr. Fujii later denied making such a statement and the newspaper retracted the report, the incident does reflect the general attitude of fear and distrust of Soka Gakkai that had developed among the Japanese by the late 1950s.*

In order to properly assess Soka Gakkai's record, however, it should be made clear that the leadership of the organization did not condone or encourage these extreme forms of shakubuku. Toda, on a number of occasions, cautioned against the use of force and violence in carrying out shakubuku activities. In an essay entitled "The Middle Path," which he wrote in 1954, Toda "appealed to his followers to be sensible in their religious fervor."[27] According to Brannen, Daisaku Ikeda, the current president of Soka Gakkai, has also appealed to members to "speak and act with common sense." Ikeda has "reprimanded them for making obscene gestures when passing before Shinto shrines and temples of other denominations. . . . And he has forbidden *shakubuku* activity on the job and frowned upon the practice of staying at a neighbor's house until the early morning hours trying to win a convert."[28]

In any objective analysis of Soka Gakkai the inescapable conclusion is that a great deal of the credit for the success of the postwar movement must go to Toda's skillful blending of organizational and doctrinal elements and to his ability as a strategist. But while Toda's contribution was of key importance, the general sociological context of the postwar period was also a factor. During the period from 1950 to 1960 a massive population migration from rural to urban areas occurred in Japanese

*For further details, see Murata, *Japan's New Buddhism,* pp. 104–5.

society. It is no coincidence that this period coincided with the first major increase in Soka Gakkai's membership. As Fujio Ikado points out, the rural to urban migration severs the migrant from traditional roots and ties. He writes that the "people who came from rural areas, and therefore were formerly in one way or another part of the traditional system of established religions, are more or less cut off from such an institution when they are in the cities. The postwar development of mass communication media has prompted the expression of individual interests and, in the course of time, the so-called 'nonreligious' people appeared openly in cities, having been released from the control of the established religion of the *ie* [literally, "house," but here meaning the extended family of traditional Japanese society] which forced belief and membership on them."[29] It was this sociological phenomenon that made the unprecedented growth of Soka Gakkai possible.

Value-Creating Pedagogy Resurrected

The central theme of the postwar movement under Toda's leadership may be symbolized by the phenomenon of shakubuku. Emphasis during this period was on the mystical and the metaphysical elements of Nichiren Shoshu, on the winning of converts to strengthen the movement, and on communicating an absolutistic message and promise of salvation that the uprooted masses of Japanese society yearned to hear. Although in guiding the movement in this direction Toda was only continuing trends and emphases that had begun under Makiguchi, the intensity and deep commitment to this direction, which came to characterize Soka Gakkai during its first decade and a half following the war, clearly reveal the imprint of Toda's personality. The implications of Toda's skillful use of ideology and organization, converging at that time with a specific psychological and sociological crisis in Japanese society, were mentioned above.

Skelton Lane suggests that the rise of social movements can be explained in terms of the interrelatedness of four major variables: leadership, ideology, organization, and what he calls structural antecedents. By structural antecedents he means some additive or cumulative process whereby multiple factors and multiple increments build up to a point at which the potential for the emergence of a social movement becomes high. At this point some precipitating factor may add the increment that makes the appearance of a social movement highly probable, whereas such a development would not have been probable or even possible at some earlier date.[30] Lane believes his analysis applies particularly to Soka Gakkai during the immediate postwar period.

With the 1960 assumption of the leadership of the organization by Daisaku Ikeda, Toda's chief disciple, a decided shift in emphasis occurred and a new dimension was added to the organization. There were numerous aspects of this shift in emphasis but in essence it may be described as a return to or a resurrection of the central elements of Makiguchi's philosophy of value and his value-creating pedagogy. It should be clear that Ikeda in no way retreated from or de-emphasized any of the elements that had characterized the organization under Toda's leadership. He continued to emphasize shakubuku both as a conversion method and as a way of life, although with some modifications; he reaffirmed the importance of repetition of the sacred prayer of Nichiren Shoshu, the daimoku, and the worship of the sect's sacred object, the mandala.*

*The importance of this worship object in Nichiren Shoshu doctrine and in the everyday worship life of Soka Gakkai members is very ably discussed in Murata, *Japan's New Buddhism,* pp. 51–52.

But alongside these mystical and doctrinal elements that had become integral aspects of the organization during Toda's administration, Ikeda added, or perhaps it would be more appropriate to say strengthened, a secular dimension of the organization.

The relationship between sacred and secular within Nichiren Shoshu Soka Gakkai is described in the religious terminology of the organization as *Rissho Ankoku* and *Obutsu Myogo*. In his presidential address to the thirty-third general meeting of the organization Ikeda clarified these concepts: "Nichiren Dai-shonin explained that *Rissho* (establishing True Buddhism) should underlie *Ankoku* (securing the peace of the land). *Rissho* means to establish True Buddhism or to achieve the unprecedented religious revolution with the life philosophy of *Shiki-shin Funi* (the inseparability of material and spiritual elements in life). This is concerned with the inner faith of the individual.

"*Ankoku* implies social prosperity, the people's happiness, and world peace. Therefore, *Rissho* is related to religion whereas *Ankoku* is applied to society. The immediate principles of *Ankoku* are the dignity of life, respect for humanity, and absolute pacifism. These are universal principles of mankind transcending religion, race, nation, and ideology. In other words, they stem from the nature of human existence. Everything is derived from this 'humanism.'

"Religion also pursues the philosophy of the nature of existence. It is the Buddhism of Nichiren Daishonin that probes this nature and substantiates it in philosophy. To believe in this Buddhism is our faith.

"In this context, *Rissho* and *Ankoku* meet in the aforementioned principles. Faith will not manifest itself directly in social activities. Instead, faith must find expression in the formation of character or in the principles such as respect for life. In this manner, faith is reflected in social activities. . . .

"So far, I have explained *Rissho Ankoku* taking politics as an example. Now, referring to *Obutsu Myogo, Rissho* (establishing True Buddhism) equals *butsu* (Buddhism) of *Obutsu,* and *Ankoku* (securing the peace of the land) means *O* (literally, king). The fusion of *O* and *butsu* is *Obutsu Myogo.*

"The Buddhist concept of *O* is the comprehensive idea of all the people and the entire society. It never means a king or state power. In our age, it means all fields of society including politics, education, and culture. Since sovereignty rests with the people today, they are kings, as is their society.

"Therefore, in the present age our activities are not limited to the political field. I would like to emphasize that this is an age in which we must build foundations in all fields of society upon which a new society and new culture should be established.

"I wish to clarify the basic difference between *Obutsu Myogo* or *Rissho Ankoku* and the unity of church and state. *Obutsu Myogo* and *Rissho Ankoku,* based on the principle of the separation of church and state, aim at forming character through religious faith and practice. They do not mean to apply faith directly to social activities. In this way, the separation of politics and religion is maintained."[31]

But while Ikeda and Soka Gakkai leaders discuss the goals of the organization in the doctrinal terminology of Buddhism, the means whereby these goals are being sought are those of Makiguchi's educational pragmatism. Satoshi Ikeda observed that Makiguchi's educational ideas have led to a revolutionary transformation in Japanese Buddhism. This transformation has been brought about by the fusion of generalized concepts of traditional Buddhism with the pragmatic educational theory and practice of Makiguchi's value-creating pedagogy.

The importance that Ikeda attached to the secular dimension became evident one year after he assumed the presidency, when, on May 3, 1961, he announced the reorganization of the

Culture Department to become the Culture Bureau, incorporating newly created departments of Economics, Politics, Education, and Speech, and later an Art Department.[32] All these departments have played significant roles in the life of the organization during the twelve-year period since the establishment of the Culture Bureau. Taken together the departments of the Culture Bureau represent a major new dimension within the new religious movements of Japanese society, a dimension that places Soka Gakkai in a separate class from the other new religions. As McFarland notes, with the exception of Soka Gakkai, none of the new religions has sought to set up organizational machinery for a sustained and purposeful involvement in the secular life of Japanese society.[33]

It is my conclusion that much of the philosophical rationale for this secular emphasis, as well as the pedagogical means for implementing it, has grown out of Ikeda's study of Makiguchi's work. Study and analysis of Makiguchi's and Ikeda's writings reveal in both a central concern for the welfare of the individual in a mass society. Out of this concern for the individual there emerges in both Makiguchi and Ikeda a common model for social reform that sees education as the key factor in the reform process. Since Makiguchi's philosophical and pedagogical ideas have been discussed at length in chapter three, in the following paragraphs this model is discussed on the basis of Ikeda's writings.

The individual as a separate, isolated unit in the midst of the mass is utterly powerless, Ikeda holds. In this powerless condition he is constantly the victim of unscrupulous individuals and pressure groups who exploit him in their own interests.[34] Ikeda believes that three things are essential if the individual is to be freed and nourished rather than destroyed by modern mass society. First of all, it is essential that each individual attain a high degree of political consciousness undergirded by a deep understanding of social structures and processes. Each such "politically conscious" and "awakened" person must then accept responsibility for keeping constant surveillance on the political process and the use of power in the society. "If true democratic politics is to be developed," Ikeda writes, "it is first necessary to clarify for the public the actual conditions of our present-day politics and then to raise the political consciousness of each citizen. Then, a watchful eye on politics will be cultivated and the bud of true democracy will emerge."[35]

Ikeda's belief that the possibility of true democracy exists only if citizens are enlightened and alert is stated even more strongly in the following paragraphs from a discussion concerning problems of modern politics: "One cannot call it an age of democracy unless the people, outside of election periods, keep a constant surveillance on politics, and the people's will is always reflected in politics. . . .

"If people elect representatives who aim at protecting only certain groups who have interests in common with their own, or if the people expect this of their representatives, confused politics will ensue and harm the entire society, hindering its constructive advance. Accordingly, the masses not only should demand their rights, but also should be awakened to their duty and responsibility in society. Only then can an ideal form of democracy be established. . . .

"These facts show that the premise of a democratic government is above all else the self-awakening of the people. They are required to have their own assertions and at the same time to listen with reason and modesty to opposing opinions, while putting into practice the merits of both. . . .

"If people lack reasonable persuasion and criticism and use the violence of the majority, they are destroying democracy with their own hands. The conflict between the majority, who disregard reason and trust in numbers, and the minority, who oppose with violence, will only result in the debasement of the democratic spirit. In this case democracy turns into mobocracy.

"Thus the position of the masses in support of democracy is very important. They are required to have a spirit of both independence and public duty, a patriotic mind, and leniency, but what is most desired of them is a good education, sound knowledge, and social morality. Whether politics improves or degrades naturally depends on whether politicians are superior or inferior. However, it is not too much to say that at the same time politics depends on the masses' intellect, culture, and moral sense. They are requested to fight resolutely against false ideas or government. That is, the masses should be self-appointed political guardians.

"From ignorance, blindness, and irresponsibility, only confusion, corruption, and disorder will be born. To blindly follow others' opinions without any consciousness or critical faculty, to abuse public rights founded in personal courtesy, to follow senselessly in response to others' movements, and to be agitated by irresponsible leaders—all these lead to destruction of democracy."[36]

One of the key elements in Ikeda's model for reform, then, as in Makiguchi's, is the alert, informed, and responsible citizen or, in Ikeda's words, the "self-appointed political guardian." The development of such politically conscious and socially responsible individuals is one of the primary tasks of education in the Soka Gakkai system under Ikeda's guidance.

The need for the development of such people in Japan is urgent, Ikeda believes, because of the degradation and corruption of Japanese political life. When one observes the condition of Japanese political life, he contends, it is easy to see how vain and empty the politicians are. Japan has, Ikeda insists, simply replaced the prewar military clique with inconsistent, corrupt, power-hungry politicians whose concerns center more in their own rather than the people's interests. "A political party in Japan is nothing but a group of political factions. . . . Cabinet posts are distributed among factions of the ruling party. The principle of putting the right man in the right place has never existed.

"Cabinet posts are coveted by Dietmen to satisfy their desire for personal fame and power. Factional leaders struggle with one another for posts to be divided among their own men. They cannot afford to concentrate their attention on alleviating the people's sufferings."[37] On the basis of such reasoning Ikeda concludes that the Japanese politician is just like a feudal lord and that democracy exists in Japan in name only.

Thus, in addition to enlightened and alert citizens, Japanese politics also needs a new breed of politician. "We are awaiting," Ikeda writes, "the appearance of fresh, reliable politicians who have undergone the human revolution and can fully satisfy the desires of the masses."[38] These new politicians will be concerned with the "rich human possibilities" of individual citizens and will base all social reforms on the premise that human society can so order itself that these human possibilities may be realized for every individual. What Japan needs, Ikeda continues, is a political party dedicated to the needs and welfare of the masses. Since none of the parties in Japan, whether conservative or reformist, filled this need, Soka Gakkai gave birth to Komeito, or the Clean Government Party, which was designed to be a party for the masses.

As Ikeda explains it: "These reformist parties, even though they promise to represent the working class, are in actuality merely the agents of 'working nobles.' They are parties for the assemblies sent by labor unions, or in other words, organizations for 'working nobles,' or labor agitators, who only aim at their own advancement in life. Accordingly, even reformist parties eixst for but a part of the people. They are degraded parties that agitate a small number of people under the name of class struggle. These parties are supported by as few people as the conservative party is. They are mere representatives of working nobles who are only a small percentage of the entire population.

"Judged on these facts, both the conservative and reformist parties are mouthpieces of minority pressure groups, or rather, are the means for assisting certain pressure groups. In Japan there are many unorganized workers in small and medium enterprises who are left untouched by politics. Still more people below those levels are utterly ignored by all the existing parties.

"A political system that is truly desirable for a mass society is one that will fill all the demands of the mass. In this respect the existing parties, which contribute merely to certain pressure groups, are all disqualified. In order to respond to public demand, they should be the parties comprising all the mass, and be firmly rooted in the complicated mass. Unless a party does truly represent the mass, the deadlock of modern society cannot be resolved. We can say that a party that is based in the masses is the new party that can powerfully promote the policies of public welfare."[39]

Ikeda further invites the people to scrutinize Komeito, while pledging that he will do the same: "Please watch Komeito activities for the next ten to twenty years. I will watch over Komeito as its supporter. But at the same time I am determined to watch all members of the Diet, including Komeito members, for any corruption and to take them to task if they are involved in corruption."[40]

The second element in Ikeda's model for social reform is that of providing the means whereby the power of the individual can be multiplied through organized cooperation with other individuals. Power must not be shunned, therefore, but actively sought so that it may be used to increase the prosperity and well-being of the entire society. This aspect of Ikeda's thought is expressed in such observations as: "We believe that democracy should be clearly distinguished from mobocracy. The ideal of democracy cannot be attained unless each individual attains a high degree of political consciousness and makes himself a humanist. In other words, democracy should not be mobocracy. Instead, it should be the government of the wise or the union of wise people."[41]

It is expressed again when Ikeda says: "The mass, separated into individuals, is utterly powerless. . . . When individuals unite in an organization and become a part of its structure, a great power is displayed. The larger the organization, the greater the role each person plays in it."[42] Thus the central issue is power and the use of power: "It is a mistake to consider power as merely evil and therefore dislike it with no reason. Rather, we must first discuss how power should be used to realize public welfare and then watch over and engage in the exercise of power."[43]

The major department in the Culture Bureau, which Ikeda created in 1961, was the Political Department. "In retrospect," Murata points out, "it is evident that the creation of the new bureau, with its Political Department, was the first step toward Soka Gakkai's full-fledged participation in the nation's politics."[44] One of the central implications of Soka Gakkai, both for its individual members and for the society of which it is a part, lies in its determination to meet the powerlessness of the individual in modern life and to influence the exercise of power in Japanese society. This feature of Soka Gakkai was present, in embryonic form, in Makiguchi's work and thought. Admittedly, it came late in his thinking; one does not find it per se in his writings. Rather, it may be inferred from his participation in the initial organization of Soka Kyoiku Gakkai in 1930, and especially in the group-oriented nature of his activities from the mid-1930s until his arrest in 1943.

This feature was also present during Toda's presidency, as a goal, a reality that must be dealt with, but without systematic or organizational expression. Satoshi Ikeda credits Toda with having said on one occasion: "Someday we have to fight with elections. So far we have prayed and engaged in shakubuku and felt that our faith was complete. This, without doubt, is basic. But the time will come when this will not be enough. To say 'I like politics' or 'I don't like politics' is irrelevant. . . . In view of the state of our country we have no choice but to step out in political life."[45] Moreover, this feature has become a major focus of Soka Gakkai's concern during the thirteen years of Ikeda's leadership.

If one fails to take into account Soka Gakkai's intentional mobilization of personal and organizational resources in order to influence and effect change in the exercise of power in Japanese society, it is impossible to understand the organization. But this is precisely the mistake that some observers of Soka Gakkai have made. For example, a *Newsweek* reporter wrote: "But what is Soka Gakkai? In its brief 33-year history, the sect has shifted doctrines so often that the only sure thing about it, aside from the lotus chant, is the sheer fact of its existence. . . . But if the past is any guide, there is no telling what position the followers of the Lotus Sutra will take next."[46]

It is not a question of whether a person approves or disapproves of this kind of exercise of power upon the part of a religious organization. The reality is that this is what Soka Gakkai seeks to do. Soka Gakkai leaders are quick to insist, however, that this does not mean religious control of the state. They are not, they contend, advocating *saisei-itchi*, or the unity of church and state. "*Obutsu Myogo* is not the 'Unity of Church and State.' In the past there were abominable relations between religion and politics. In medieval Christianity, religious authorities ruled politics, or political power utilized religion. . . . This should not be confused with *Obutsu Myogo*. If a religion is

forced on the masses by the government or by law, of what use
will it be? It means the impotence of the religion, its isolation
from the masses, and the loss of its eternity."[47] Elsewhere Ikeda
argues that "*saisei-itchi* is an ancient form of government in
which one and the same person is in charge of both religious
rites and politics. If this primitive form of theocracy were to be
realized by Soka Gakkai, we would have to entreat the high
priest of Nichiren Shoshu to become prime minister."[48] But
such assurances notwithstanding, some observers both in Japan
and in other countries continue to be skeptical of Soka Gakkai
on this point. The fact remains that under Ikeda's leadership
Soka Gakkai, by building on the spirit and further developing
the implications of Makiguchi's educational philosophy and
pedagogy, is creating new social structures that give promise of
radically altering interrelationships among education, religion,
politics, and society in Japan.

The third element in Ikeda's model for social reform is the
most basic and the one on which the other two elements depend
for their meaning. It is the proposition that society must be
so ordered as to provide for the maximum growth and development of every individual in the society. Phrased in Soka Gakkai's
terminology, it means that developing people capable of
creating value and providing opportunity for such people to
give expression to their creativity are central objectives of the
organization. For Soka Gakkai this is more than window dress-
ing. Soka Gakkai, Ikeda claims, is committed and dedicated to
the improvement and change of society in the interests of
all of society's members, rather than in the interests of a specific
class or group. Ikeda insists that one all-important criterion
must guide every aspect of social planning and political action;
namely, the question of how any plan or action will affect the
individual members of society. All social plans and every
political action must be subjected to the test of the extent to
which they contribute toward the end of enabling every mem-

ber of society to become fulfilled, value-creating individuals.

This brings one back to a central theme in Makiguchi's thought, that of the dual personal-social nature of man, and the need for a harmonious balance within every person's life between the pursuit of values of personal gain and the pursuit of values of social good. One cannot, in other words, be a complete, happy, value-creating person by himself. Only as he senses his interconnection with other people in a social matrix and seeks to create values that will bring about the fulfillment and happiness of these other lives, as well as his own, is happiness or fulfillment possible for him. This basic view of Makiguchi's is today expressed by Ikeda and Soka Gakkai as the goal to seek social salvation and prosperity through the attainment of each individual's happiness. Ikeda says that "priority should be given to man's right to live, and respect for humanity should be placed above all else. The ideal public welfare, which aims at 'social prosperity in accordance with individual happiness,' should be the goal of politics."[49] However, he continues: "The actual situation is far from ideal. Rather, it is common that social prosperity is separated from individual happiness. To bring about a change in this situation presents the greatest problem of our present-day politics."[50]

Like Makiguchi prior to his preoccupation with religious concerns, Ikeda sees education as the single most important factor in changing the present reality. Value-creating people dedicated to the task of ordering society in such a way as to attain both "social prosperity and individual happiness" do not just spring up automatically. Educational systems that have individual and social value-creativity as their central goal have to give birth to them. Toward this end, Makiguchi developed his value-creating pedagogy. Also toward this end, Ikeda, since assuming the presidency of Soka Gakkai, has moved consistently to implement the principles of value-creating pedagogy. His latest effort in this regard has been the establishment of formal educational institutions. Soka High School was opened with the enrollment of seventh- and tenth-grade classes on April 8, 1968.* Soka University enrolled its first classes in April, 1971. On May 28 the *Japan Times* said of the new university: "The Sokagakkai, one of the most influential religious organizations in Japan for the past several decades, has now launched a new venture in the field of education. Soka University, an institution that may well be setting a new trend for the educational system of Japan, started classes last April near Hachioji City some 30 miles west of Tokyo. . . .

"At present about 700 students, of which over 100 are coeds, are attending the new university. . . . Student enrollment will be increased to 8,000 in the near future.

"The student-faculty ratio at the university is presently 5 to 1 but the ratio will be stabilized to around 15 to 1 for maximum results. This is almost unheard of in present Japanese universities.

"The university includes a complete dormitory system for faculties and the university staff members as well as all students. This is to foster a closer relationship between students and faculty as well as to help students develop self-reliance and autonomy and to encourage them to experience cooperative group life. . . .

"The idea of Soka University was proposed by Daisaku Ikeda, president of Sokagakkai, at the 7th general meeting of the organization's student division. Ikeda was dissatisfied with the present educational system of mass education and decided to set up a school which puts more emphasis on personal relations between faculty and students, combined with the best modern facilities available.

"The late Tsunesaburo Makiguchi, first president of Sokagak-

*For an excellent description and discussion of the Soka High School, see Carl H. Gross, *Soka Gakkai and Education* (East Lansing: Michigan State University, Institute for International Studies, 1970), pp. 56–63.

kai, established the unique Soka Educational Theory upon whose basic tenets lies the educational foundation of the university. His principle—'Education should aim at creating values in one's character.'

"Kazuo Takamatsu, president of the university, announced the motto which reflects Makiguchi's as well as Ikeda's philosophy: The highest institution of human education, the cradle of a new culture, and the fortress of peace for mankind."

Ikeda indicated his views of the need for and importance of Soka University in an address to the thirty-first general meeting of Soka Gakkai in May, 1968: "Needless to say, education is the most important undertaking that will determine the future of Japan and the trend of the world. So far, however, politicians and leaders of our country have been all too indifferent to this problem. Moreover, there seem to be signs of intensified intervention in various ways with an ulterior motive of exploiting education as a tool of political struggle. If things are left as they are, I am gravely worried that university education will inevitably lose its dignity further and become confused and enervated.

"Under the circumstances, I cannot help being convinced that it is our Soka Gakkai—living in the tradition of deep thought and practice formed by our founder-president Tsunesaburo Makiguchi and by former president Josei Toda—and our Soka University that have the true qualifications and mission to translate the ideal form of education into reality and to drastically change the stance of educational circles. In particular, the university must be the mother of both a nation's culture and the crystallization of a nation's spirit."[51]

It is too early at this point to attempt to assess the long-range outcome of Soka Gakkai's efforts. There should be no misunderstanding, however, as to what those efforts consist of. Soka Gakkai, as suggested earlier, has set out to permanently rearrange the power balance and influence the exercise of power in

Japanese society. The restructuring of formal education in accordance with the principles of Makiguchi's value-creating pedagogy is seen as a necessary and basic step toward achieving the organization's objectives. Murata has insightfully observed that today, forty years after Makiguchi's own attempts to reform Japanese education ended in failure, Soka Gakkai "has an opportunity to put the late founder's educational theory into practice on a grand scale."[52]

5 *Education in a Self-Renewing Society*

A Frame of Reference

Any attempt to assess an individual's or movement's contribution to society and culture, if the assessment is to be meaningful beyond the particular case, must necessarily include some theoretical frame of reference with regard to social behavior and interaction within which the life and behavior of the individual or movement can be understood and interpreted. This is not to say that the historian must be an anthropologist or sociologist. As a historian he is concerned with analyzing the actions of a particular person or a set of events or processes. As a historian he must remain close to the "actual happenings and avoid statements which, though linking behavior at one time or place to that elsewhere, lead to a distortion in the description of what occurred in the set of circumstances being analyzed."[1]

The anthropologist and the sociologist, however, look for concepts that subsume a variety of particular descriptive categories. These anthropological and sociological concepts provide the historian sets of categories and frames of reference to order historical materials with, and these categories and frames of reference may enhance the power of his interpretive or causal explanation.[2] If the historian has profited from contributions of the anthropologist and the sociologist, they, at the same time, have come to recognize the value of historical evidence in their own research. This recognition has within the past decade led to the reemergence of historical and comparative studies within the fields of anthropology and sociology as valid and valued areas of inquiry. The prospects appear good, therefore, for the development of fruitful cooperation between historians, on the one hand, and anthropologists and sociologists, on the other. The historian can contribute to such interdisciplinary endeavor by utilizing anthropological and sociological concepts in ordering and conducting his research and by reporting his findings in such a way that they will be usable and available for comparative study by social scientists.

The theory of social and cultural change formulated by the anthropologist Anthony F. C. Wallace was selected as a theoretical frame of reference for this examination of Makiguchi and the Soka Gakkai movement. Wallace's theory is particularly relevant for this purpose because both education and revolutionary movements, such as Soka Gakkai, are treated as major conceptual variables. Wallace holds that study and analysis of the learning process in any human society may be approached with a two-dimensional model.

The first dimension concerns the circumstances in which the learning process occurs. Wallace arranges the circumstances of human learning in the form of a scale of generality, each category of which is contained in and implied by its succeeding category. Schooling, his first category, is followed by education, enculturation, and finally learning itself. Schooling is learning done in a school. A school is defined as "an institution which deliberately and systematically, by the presentation of symbols in reading matter, lectures, or ritual, attempts to transform from a condition of ignorance to one of enlightenment, the intellect, the morality, and the technical knowledge and skills of an attentive group of persons assembled in a definite place at a definite time."[3] Education is "all learning (including but not confined to schooling) obtained from reading or from listening to formally prepared symbolic presentations."[4] Enculturation is "all learning enjoined on the person with a particular status as a member of a particular culture-bearing society, and thus includes, in addition to schooling and education, such homely but essential skills as knowing a language or two; observing the proper times, places, and techniques for the execution of such malleable body processes as urination, defecation, breathing, walking, eating, sleeping, and sexual intercourse."[5] Learning is the cover term and embraces "all of the foregoing, and also those idiosyncratic learnings which every person accumulates throughout his lifetime and which may or may not be transmitted to others."[6]

The second dimension of Wallace's model classifies learning by matter rather than by position on a scale of circumstances. Thus, according to Wallace, in any situation of learning three matters may be learned. These are matters of technic, of morality, and of intellect. Technic is "how to" learning by reinforcement: "It includes such things as learning how to talk, how to extract the square root of a number, how to dance, how to harpoon a walrus, . . . how to identify a witch, how to get to heaven. From this standpoint, even the rote learning of information—dates, names, events, formulas, art work, institutional structures, store prices, fashions, and the like—is 'how to' learning, for the motive lies not in the acquisition of the information but in the use to which it may be put. . . . And even values—such as standards of beauty, tastes in music, concepts of the good life—may be learned, both by rote, as when one learns first the symbols for the rewarded values, and later, by performing the act that earns the reward."[7]

Morality, however, deals not so much with "how to" as with "what." Furthermore, in Wallace's usage, morality concerns "not just positive and negative goals, not just values, not even all socially approved values, but one particular kind of socially approved value. This kind of value is the conception that one's own behavior, as well as the behavior of others, should not merely take into consideration the attitude of the community, but should actively advance, or at least not retard, its welfare. Morality is thus to be sharply distinguished from mere propriety, conformity, and respectability, although it is not necessarily non-conformist. Morality, in this sense, is most conspicuously exemplified by such heroic actions as the soldier's who throws himself on a hand grenade in order to smother the blast and save his buddies. . . .

"It is, to my way of thinking, questionable whether this kind of morality can be adequately explained by any simple learning-by-reinforcement model. Although morality is not necessarily accompanied by sacrifice, in any particular case its criterion is its potentiality for sacrifice. And sacrifice seems to fly in the face of the law of effect. Indeed, the American academic psychologist is apt to deny that moral behavior in this sense can exist in a sane person. . . . Yet anyone who has observed men in combat, who has seen the religious or the political devotee in action, who has watched a family holding together in adversity, must realize that morally altruistic behavior is possible. And it is hard to escape the inference that such persons, on such occasions, have not learned to sacrifice their own interests in favor of their conception of the interests of other persons merely by passing through some adroitly arranged sequence of Skinner boxes."[8]

Intellect is not the same as intelligence, nor is it intellectualism. Rather, intellect, in Wallace's usage, refers to a social tradition, an aspect of culture, the core of which involves the proposition that if a subject is worthy of consideration at all it should be considered in a particular cognitive form. Wallace seems to be referring here to principles of critical thinking or what in John Dewey's terminology would be the scientific method or problem-solving approach to learning. The utility of intellect, Wallace writes, "springs from the fact that it is the only truly universal tool, capable of maintaining and restoring human arrangements against the erosions of time, capable of recognizing and solving new problems as well as learning the answers to old ones. And it does this intensely human task by requiring its users to practice what is sometimes, and paradoxically, described as an inhuman detachment from the technics and morality of the moment."[9]

Wallace suggests the diagram in Figure 1[10] to represent the divisions of learning discussed thus far, that is, the three matters of learning, as well as the scale of the circumstances of learning.

The key educational issue that faces the people of every society is concerned with the question, What should a man learn? Societies differ in their answer to this question; and these differences, Wallace theorizes, can be related to the particular value orientation of a society. While the values that guide a society in its choices of what learnings to impress on the individual are legion, and while these may be described on many levels of complexity, Wallace suggests that any society

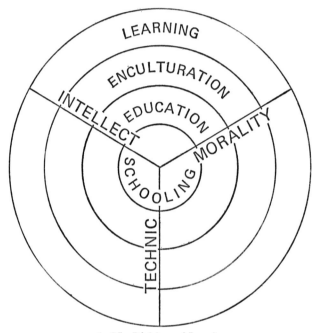

1. The Divisions of Learning

can be explained and understood with reference to one or a combination of three contrasting value orientations. These are the revolutionary, or utopian, orientation; the conservative, or ideological, orientation; and the reactionary orientation. What a man is expected to do in his life will, in part, depend on "whether he lives in a revolutionary, conservative, or reactionary society. And what he is expected to do determines what he is expected to learn. Furthermore, not merely what a man should learn, but whether he should learn it in a school, or from his parents, or from his peers, or by casual reading, conversation, and attendance at entertainments, will be in part determined by whether he lives in a revolutionary or a conservative or a reactionary society."[11]

While in reality no society could be wholly one or another of these three types, it seems reasonable to consider one value orientation or another predominant in a given group, such as the political, economic, or religious leadership of a society, during a given period. This tripartite classification may be used also for the different time periods in the same society. Wallace believes that we may expect that these orientations will change in a definite order. Thus, "a society which is now revolutionary will, if it changes, become conservative, next reactionary, and again most probably revolutionary."[12] What Wallace is suggesting here, then, is that over centuries and millennia any given society "is apt to follow a roughly cyclical path through revolution, conservatism, and reaction, over and over again."[13] The specific conceptual tool used by Wallace to study this phenomenon is what he defines as a "revitalization movement."

Wallace's general theory may be summarized by noting that with regard to any one society, we may expect to find that both the content and the circumstances of learning will vary with the changing predominance of its value orientation. More specifically, it would appear "that with each of the major value orientations there is associated a philosophy of schooling which characteristically assigns priorities to the matters of learning in schools."[14]

Revitalization Movements, Educational Priorities, and Value Orientations

Analysis of the association between these priorities and the value orientations represents the major thrust of Wallace's theoretical formulation. A revolutionary society, thus, is a society that is dominated by a revitalization movement. A revitalization movement is defined as "a deliberate, organized, conscious effort by members of a society to construct a more satisfying culture."[15] A revitalization movement may in the extreme be either religious or political but is usually a combination of both. The code of a revitalization movement "defines the previous state of society as inadequate, perverse, even evil, and depicts a more or less utopian image of the better society as the goal culture toward which the *ad hoc* and temporary social arrangements of the present transfer culture is carrying the society."[16]

A revitalization movement generally has six tasks to perform or six stages that it must pass through in order to create a truly revolutionary society. These stages are:

"Formulation of the code. Mere dissatisfaction with the existing state of affairs does not launch a revitalization movement. A prophet, political party, or clique must formulate explicitly the nature of the existing culture's deficiencies, the nature of a desirable goal culture, and the nature and mode of operation of the transfer culture. This formulation must be more than an exercise of intellect; it must be passionately moral.

"Communication. The formulator must preach his code to other people. This communication must emphasize the moral obligation of the bearer to subscribe to this new code and render service to the movement.

"Organization. The converts made by the formulator organize into a hierarchical system, with a prophet or other titular head, an elite group of disciples who constitute an executive praesidium, and a rank and file who carry out but do not make policy.

"Adaptation. As the movement's challenge to the existing leadership of the society is met, by counter-propaganda or by

force, the movement will be required to enlarge, modify, specify, and otherwise adapt the code to the circumstances of survival. The process of reformulation is continuous from this point on, for new situations constantly arise not anticipated in the code; and it lasts long after political victory is complete. This process of doctrinal elaboration is a work of disciplined intellect, and high value is accordingly placed on intellect, which can perform such work (whereas technic cannot).

"Cultural transformation. When social power falls into the hands of the movement (the revolution is 'won'), the movement is able to carry out directly the cultural transformation of the society. In this process, morality and intellect are more valuable than technic, for technic tends to be conservative, and intellect will discern that a new technic will have to be invented to meet new tasks.

"Routinization. As the movement's immediate aims are realized by the acquisition of power and the establishment, if not of the goal culture, at least of the transfer culture, the organization of the movement *per se* tends to contract into the form of a church, or a behind-the-scenes party, which attempts to maintain the ongoing transfer culture. At this point the society has become conservative, with a division of role between the executive and the morality-maintaining functions."[17]

The main point to be noted with respect to schools and schooling is that in a revolutionary society the primary concern of the schools must be the moral transformation of the population. Next in importance is intellect and last is technic. "The reason for this priority list—morality, intellect, and technic—is that the moral rebirth of the population and the development of a cadre of morally reliable and intellectually resourceful individuals to take over executive positions throughout the society is the immediately necessary task."[18]

A conservative society is a society that has won its battle with reaction and has established a successful new culture. The new culture, although it may be in some cases only a transfer culture rather than the goal culture itself, has become secure; thus the old movement does not need to preoccupy itself with combat against reaction or against new revitalization movements. "The problem is to keep the machine going as efficiently as possible, with occasional improvements, and possibly with smoothly programmed shifts from one stage to another on the path toward the goal culture."[19] In contrast to the revolutionary society, the conservative society is not primarily concerned with morality. This is because the transformation of the society is sufficiently complete for severe moral nonconformists to be treated as delinquents, criminals, or victims of mental illness. "The reform, rehabilitation, or control of these people can be safely left to the police, the courts, or the medical profession, and (most importantly) to the informal sanctions of the family and the community itself."[20] It is even possible, Wallace observes, for a conservative society to permit a degree of open nonconformity. A conservative society is, he says, "paradoxically, also a liberal society, precisely because the elite is secure enough that it can afford to learn from its critics and even absorb them into the ranks of conservatism as a 'loyal opposition.' "[21]

Intellect is valued least in a conservative society. The work of code formulation and its application have been accomplished; thus the skilled practitioner of intellect is not necessary to the regime: "Intellect becomes a rather special tradition, relatively free from constraint, but without access to power because, in a political sense, it has little power to offer. Thus the schools see relatively little need to force intellect even upon the intelligent. Intellect becomes a career in itself, self-sought and guild-protected, with the members of the guild practicing partly for the fun of it and partly as professional men selling their services to the highest bidder."[22]

Technic, then, becomes the first concern of the conservative society, and the primary concern of the school. The school, as C. Wright Mills has observed with reference to the United States, first of all trains people to do jobs.[23] Morality comes next in importance for it is considered, in a negative sort of way, to be necessary to keep society from falling apart. Intellect is placed last. While it may be respected, it also tends to be viewed with suspicion and distrust.

The reactionary society is a postconservative society. The conservative order, "having been challenged by a budding revitalization movement (i.e., by what it regards as a treasonable heretical conspiracy imported from abroad), adjusts its posture to minimize the effectiveness of its competitors' propaganda and to mobilize counter-attacks. In the interest of preserving the same values that an earlier revitalization movement established in pain and sweat, and which the conservative society cherished and elaborated, the reactionary society subverts its own way of life in order to deliver telling blows against the enemy within. In so doing it may destroy the very social structure which it is defending; and it becomes, because of the growing discrepancy between ideal and practice, and because popular confidence in its values begins to erode, rapidly moribund, an eminent subject for revitalization."[24]

In the area of learning, two concerns predominate in the reactionary society. One is "to combat the alien heresies by revealing the inadequacy of their values and the poverty of their practice," and the other is "to recapture the moral enthusiasm of its earlier, revitalization phase."[25] In other words, the reactionary society shares with the revolutionary society a deep concern for morality, but for different reasons. In the logic of revolution, Wallace writes, "morality and intellect are believed to be linked in a pact with the future. Hence . . . the revolutionary society will place intellect before technic in its scale of priority: the cultivation of intellect becomes a kind of capital investment in people. In the reactionary society, by contrast, intellect is feared as a potential enemy because, in the preceding conservative phase, it has acted as endowed critic of the conventional wisdom. . . . Thus the reactionary society will favor technic over intellect. . . . The ultimate consequence to a reactionary society of neglecting the cultivation of intellect is collapse before the onslaught of a revitalization movement which is guided by intellect."[26]

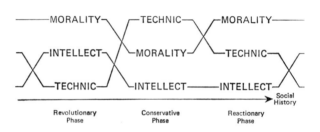

2. *The Matters of Learning*

Figure 2[27] displays the comparison of value orientations and associated priorities of the matters of learning according to Wallace's theory.

―――――――――― *Prophet of a Revitalization Movement*

Analysis of Makiguchi's life and thought within the theoretical context provided by Wallace suggests that Makiguchi was, in fact, a dynamic prophet of a significant revitalization movement in Japanese society. As pointed out in chapter one, Japanese society during the period roughly from 1890 to the beginning of

World War II was experiencing a continuous battle for control between revolutionary and reactionary forces. But while this battle continued to be waged, it was fought on very unequal terms, for the reactionary elements had won the battle to all intents and purposes in 1889 and 1890. The constitution of 1889 was the official declaration of the reactionary success. The Imperial Rescript on Education of 1890 spelled out the implications of that success for the Japanese school system. In the scheme outlined in the rescript morality was of paramount importance, technic was second, and intellect was last.

In the midst of this situation Makiguchi initiated a new revitalization movement based, not on Western technical knowledge as had been the case with the earlier revitalization movement that had carried off the Meiji Restoration in 1868, but on educational principles, concepts, and practices gleaned primarily from western-European and American educational pragmatism as expressed in the works of John Dewey and Lester Ward. Makiguchi's movement built slowly. For nearly half a century Makiguchi was a voice in the wilderness, participating as an educator in Japanese society but at the same time highly critical of its values and particularly of its educational practices. During this period Makiguchi worked at the formulation of a new cultural code, pinpointing the inadequacies of Japanese education and society as he saw them, hammering out the dimensions of a goal culture, as well as the nature and mode of operation of a transfer culture.

Each of these three aspects of code formulation can be clearly seen in the discussion of Makiguchi's educational philosophy and practice in chapters three and four. It will be worth noting in more detail, however, certain features of his approach to the development and operation of a transfer culture. Wallace indicates that there are two variables involved here: the amount of secular action that takes place in a movement, and the amount of religious action. He says: "Secular action here is defined as the manipulation of human relationships; religious action as the manipulation of relationships between human and supernatural beings. No revitalization movement can, by definition, be truly nonsecular, but some can be relatively less religious than others, and movements can change in emphasis depending on changing circumstances. There is a tendency . . . for movements to become more political in emphasis, and to act through secular rather than religious institutions, as problems of organization, adaptation, and routinization become more pressing."[28]

Makiguchi initially envisioned a purely secular movement. His emphasis was on the manipulation of human relationships through restructuring the educational system and substituting alternative methods and values. When his initial efforts to develop a transfer culture based on this model were throttled by the military-reactionary coalition, which got the upper hand in Japanese society in the 1930s, Makiguchi, aided by religious ideas recently acquired through his conversion to Nichiren Shoshu, shifted his strategy to include a transfer culture based predominantly on religious action. Viewed within this framework, both Makiguchi's seeming turnabout from a strictly pragmatic orientation to an absolutistic one and the religious fanaticism that characterized the final years of his life appear more understandable.

The effect of Makiguchi's shift from secular to religious means of attaining the goals of his movement was to bring about a reordering of priorities of the matters of learning in the movement itself. Initially, Makiguchi's value-creating pedagogy sought to reorder the priorities of the matters of learning in Japan's reactionary society, placing intellect first in importance, morality second, and technic third. For example, see his objectives in community study outlined in chapter three and his proposal for a half-day school plan. At a later stage in the life of the movement and associated with the shift to religious action, concern for morality and commitment became paramount; intellect reverted to secondary importance, with technic third. Thus, at this stage, Makiguchi's movement corresponded to Wallace's ideal revitalization movement in a revolutionary society. The movement was just beginning to enjoy success when its back was broken and its members were dispersed by action of the government in the early 1940s.

The postwar movement that developed under Toda's leadership continued the revolutionary characteristics of the prewar movement; i.e., morality continued to be of first importance, with intellect second, and technic third. A further interesting phenomenon has become evident since the leadership of the movement passed to Daisaku Ikeda in 1960. While Ikeda has continued to place strong emphasis on morality and moral training, he has proceeded to attach increasing importance to the role of intellect in the movement. In this respect he appears to be much more like Makiguchi than was Toda.

This tendency of Ikeda's to elevate intellect to a higher priority among the matters of learning raises some interesting questions concerning revitalization movements and their role in cultural change. Wallace suggests, to review briefly the central points of our theoretical orientation, that there occur in human societies cyclical processes of cultural change, the major phases of which are revolution, conservatism, and reaction. A key factor in these cyclical processes is the revitalization movement. Thus one can expect that the future of any given society will inevitably hold within it this cyclical process, i.e., the coalescing of dissatisfied individuals in a society into a revitalization movement (or movements), the striving for and in some cases capturing of power by a revitalization movement, the development of a conservative society based on the new code and value orientation of the revitalization movement, the eventual development of a reactionary movement that comes into being to counter new revitalization movements and to preserve the values of the conservative society inherited from an earlier revitalization movement, the eventual collapse of the reactionary movement before the onslaught of a revitalization movement that is guided by intellect, and thus the cycle repeats itself. While this general theoretical formulation is extremely helpful in analyzing cultural and social change, there are some questions that may be raised with regard to it. First of all, the obvious may be noted; this theory is based on study and analysis of past and presently existing societies. Secondly, this theory seems to assume that human societies inherently have a particular type of composition, i.e., a ruling elite that dominates and exploits a poorly educated mass that is susceptible to and receptive of the propaganda disseminated by the elite group to justify its domination of the society. This theory does not appear to grant the possibility of a society without ruling elites and with competent citizenry. Finally, this theory appears to limit the possible range in the ordering of priorities to the three that have been found to correspond to the revolutionary, the conservative, and the reactionary value orientations. There would seem to be room to question some of these assumptions.

What would be the consequences for instance, if a revitalization movement, rather than following the usual tendency of such movements to order priorities of the matters of learning as morality, intellect, and technic, were to hold intellect to be first in importance, morality second, and technic third? Frankly, we do not know. While such ordering has been proposed, we cannot point to any revitalization movements that have succeeded on the basis of this ordering of priorities. This was, in effect, as noted above, the ordering of priorities in Makiguchi's initial movement, based on his value-creating pedagogy, prior to the shift to religious action during the 1930s. But more significantly, it appears to describe the present ordering of priorities within Soka Gakkai. There is no mistaking the fact that under Ikeda's leadership the primary concern for morality, which characterized Soka Gakkai during Toda's regime, has yielded to emphasis upon intellect. While morality is still considered to be of critical importance, it is now secondary.

The present ordering of priorities within Soka Gakkai may have far-reaching significance. It should be recognized, first of all, that this ordering of priorities brings into being a new relationship between a revitalization movement and the general population of the society in which it was given birth. Note again what Wallace says with respect to schools and schooling in a revolutionary society: "One inference is paramount: that in a revolutionary society (i.e., a society in the process of cultural transformation under the leadership of a revitalization movement) the primary concern of schools must be the moral transformation of the population. Next in order of priority will be intellect; and last of all, technic (despite the often critical need for technically trained personnel to carry out the program of the transfer culture). The reason for this priority list—morality, intellect, technic—is that the moral rebirth of the population and the development of a cadre of morally reliable and resourceful individuals to take over executive positions throughout the society is the immediately necessary task."[29]

In the revolutionary society described by Wallace the movement leadership sees the mass primarily as potential support in the movement's effort to seize power and establish itself in the society. In other words, the revolutionary revitalization movement's interest in the individuals making up the mass of the society's population stems from a desire for converts, or to put it more graphically, for bodies. Little concern or thought is given to the nature or characteristics of those bodies so long as training in morality can make them loyal supporters of the movement's cause and so long as training in intellect can enable them to sufficiently comprehend the philosophical rationale of the movement so they can be persuasive recruiters for it and so some of them can become competent executers of its will.

I submit that this relationship between the revolutionary revitalization movement and the mass of people in the society in which the movement is operating inevitably leads to the movement's downfall or, to use Wallace's terminology, to its becoming conservative if it succeeds as a revitalization movement. The important thing to recognize here is the crucial role of formal education and the ordering of its priorities. Thus it is being suggested that the cycles of revolution, conservatism, and reaction, which Wallace rightly sees occurring, do not occur because such a cyclical process is inherent within human social interaction. They occur, rather, as a result of the almost universal tendency, up to now, for revitalization movements to give first priority to morality. In doing so, as Wallace notes, they link morality and intellect in a pact with the future. The future, be it noted, however, refers not to the future of humanity nor to the welfare of the society as a whole, but to the future of the revitalization movement itself, i.e., the preservation of the movement for the movement's sake. Interesting in this respect is John Gardner's observation that revolutionaries very often prove to be more rigid and uncreative than the forces they are opposing.[30] In the same vein Arthur Koestler says that "if we survey history and compare the lofty aims, in the name of which revolutions were started, and the sorry end to which they came, we see again and again how a polluted civilization pollutes its own revolutionary offspring."[31]

In contrast, Soka Gakkai, in choosing to give intellect top priority, may be pointing toward a more permanent solution to human problems. In effect, Soka Gakkai seems to be saying that as important as training in morality is, training in intellect is even more important. In the revolutionary revitalization movement intellect is pressed into the service of the movement. A marriage is consummated between intellect and morality, as Wallace puts it, toward the end of consolidating and establishing the movement's morality. In Soka Gakkai, however, under Ikeda's leadership, intellect is not pressed into the service of the movement, but rather is aimed at transforming the quality of mind of the entire population, equipping that population to judge the movement and to hold both it and its competitors accountable.

Two references that deal either directly or indirectly with the question of intellect being given priority over morality are worth noting at this point. One is Lester Ward's sociological theory and his concept of sociocracy that, as noted earlier, was a significant influence in the development of Makiguchi's own thought. Ward insisted that education, which to him meant the "universal diffusion of scientific knowledge," must underlie all social reform.[32] The other reference is Michael Harrington's *Accidental Century*. Harrington holds that during the past century mankind has blindly stumbled through an "accidental revolution." He contends that the only hope for man's survival, as an individual with dignity and personal worth, is to make this revolution conscious and democratic rather than unconscious and accidental.

Soka Gakkai may well be breaking open new frontiers in this respect. As indicated earlier, while this ordering of priorities, i.e., intellect, morality, and technic, has been advocated before (it was the major import of Dewey's thought, as well as of Makiguchi's), no revitalization movement to date has taken the idea seriously enough to commit itself to testing its validity. The progressive education movement in America, for example, did not really deal with the central issues in Dewey's thought. Yet a strong case can be made for the need for such testing. Wallace himself, for instance, raises questions about the inevitability of the cyclical process of which he writes, and he admits the possibility of additional alternatives in the ordering of priorities: "Let me suggest what, in a conservative society [the United States] intending to survive in a revolutionary world by refusing to freeze into the reactionary posture, the value hierarchy of the schools should be. The cultivation of intellect should come first, technic second, and morality last."[33]

Wallace does not give reasons for listing technic above morality. The main point, however, is his suggestion that raising training in intellect to first priority may be so important as to be a question of survival. Here Wallace is in general agreement with the direction in which Soka Gakkai seems to be going: "This to my mind is the kind of thing that intellect is all about. Intellect is a cultural matter; it must be learned; and, for survival, it must be used. Our country's survival as a conservative society—or, indeed, as any kind of society—depends radically upon maintaining a system of schools which teaches the tradition of intellect as its primary obligation."[34] It seems almost unnecessary to mention at this point, but perhaps one should do so in order to avoid any misunderstanding, that Wallace does not mean by intellect the memorization of factual information unrelated to the life of the learner. He does not even refer to acquiring skills in the three R's, although he does not exclude those skills. He refers, rather, to a grasp or comprehension of the meaning of life lived in society. He refers to the acquisition of skills in reasoning, analyzing, comparing, questioning. He refers to "problem solving" as Dewey used that concept.

The carrying out within society of an ordering of priorities that places intellect first has been and is being called for by many other writers and educators. Mention can be made here of only a few of them. No one has stated the case for intellect more clearly than Arthur Koestler in his novel *Darkness at Noon*. In a reflection on the plight of some of his characters Koestler writes that "a people's capacity to govern itself democratically is . . . proportionate to the degree of its understanding of the structure and functioning of the whole social body."[35]

More recently Suzanne Keller has pointed out the dangers inherent in an uninformed and socially incompetent and irresponsible mass population: "A . . . graver danger lies in the informational gap between specialized leaders and the public, a gap that nullifies many of the rights available to the public on paper. Ignorance of the public often encourages leaders to resort to irrational methods of persuasion and communication. In an age of mass communications, the power of leaders to manipulate public opinion is extraordinary. 'The spectacle of an efficient elite maintaining its authority and asserting its will over the mass by the rationally calculated use of irrational methods of persuasion is the most disturbing nightmare of mass democracy.' The best safeguard against this danger is for the public to become literate, informed, and thus potentially critical of decisions and proposals made by leaders."[36]

C. Wright Mills called attention to the confusion and the sense of being trapped that is felt by modern men. Ordinary men, he wrote, "do not possess the quality of mind essential to grasp the interplay of man and society, of biography and history, of self and world. They cannot cope with their personal troubles in such ways as to control the structural transformations that usually lie behind them. . . .

"What they need, and what they feel they need, is a quality of mind that will help them to use information and to develop reason in order to achieve lucid summations of what is going on in the world and what may be happening within themselves."[37]

This capacity of an individual to understand himself in relation to his society, the capacity to locate oneself within one's period of history, Mills refers to as the "sociological imagination": "What we experience in various and specific milieux, I have noted, is often cause by structural changes. Accordingly, to understand the changes of many personal milieux we are required to look beyond them. And the number and variety of such structural changes increases as the institutions within which we live become more embracing and more intricately connected with one another. To be aware of the idea of social structure and to use it with sensibility is to be capable of tracing such linkages among a great variety of milieux. To be able to do that is to possess the sociological imagination."[38]

Several modern writers have insisted, with Makiguchi, Dewey, and Ikeda, that if man is to deal successfully with the new world he has inherited, he must give attention to urgent needs in the field of education. Shortly before her death in November, 1962, Eleanor Roosevelt wrote: "If we are to cope successfully with our revolutions in science, in the economy, in social areas, we must prepare for the revolution in education that will be required to meet, to understand, and to master the new conditions. Without a totally new approach to education our young people are not going to be equipped to cope with the world of the future."[39]

William Drake has expressed a belief that the future of our modern, technological society may well depend on the development of the kind of awareness and understanding envisioned in the sociological imagination and the use of such awareness and understanding in social engineering.[40] However, he contends, individuals with such understanding and the will to use it on behalf of a total society's welfare can only be produced by certain kinds of educational experiences. In Drake's view such educational experiences must be characterized by dialogue. Because his conclusions speak so directly to the issues considered here they are quoted at length: "In our analysis . . . we have been operating on the assumption that the growth of the thought processes was at the heart of an educa-

tional program adequate to a free society. It is our conviction
that the history of social thought and modern studies in child
growth support this assumption. In this respect the Socratic
as contrasted with the catechetical method stands out with
striking superiority. In the development of the human mind,
man did not start with a catechism, but with a dialogue of
speech and gesture between mother and child. . . .

"The civilization of the dialogue lies at the heart of the
life of a free people, but to what extent do we find the qualities
necessary to carry on this democratic process in operation in
the social and cultural agencies of the United States today?
. . . 'Civilization of the Dialogue' seems to have been first
used by Kierkegaard to characterize the growth of parlia-
mentary democracy, but the idea is as old as ancient Greece
and was used by Homer in the debates between the gods and
the Athenians. Christian dogmatism (the catechism) and the
loss of a sense of creativity among men led to the demise of the
concept until modern times. . . . Of prime and lasting significance to the upgrading of the educative effort and to the
endurance of a free society is a deeper concern for and an
implementation of the 'Civilization of the Dialogue.' "[41]

Perhaps better than any other contemporary educator, John
Gardner, in his concept of the renewal of people and societies,
has pulled together the essential relationships between education and society being discussed here. With language sounding
very much like that of Makiguchi, Gardner notes that "all
too often we are giving our young people cut flowers when we
should be teaching them to grow their own plants. We are
stuffing their heads with the products of earlier innovation
rather than teaching them to innovate. We think of the mind
as a storehouse to be filled when we should be thinking of it
as an instrument to be used."[42]

However, Gardner believes that we "are moving away from
teaching things that readily become outmoded, and toward

things that will have the greatest long-term effect on the young person's capacity to understand and perform. Increasing emphasis is being given to instruction in methods of analysis and modes of attack on problems."[43] In the long run, Gardner concludes, the school system is probably the most effective means of bringing about in our society the changes that our time demands. Thus education (formal schooling) "can lay a broad and firm base for a lifetime of learning and growth. The individual who begins with such a broad base will always have some capacity to function as a generalist, no matter how deeply he chooses to specialize. Education at its best will develop the individual's inner resources to the point where he can learn (and will want to learn) on his own. It will equip him to cope with unforeseen challenges and to survive as a versatile individual in an unpredictable world. Individuals so educated will keep the society itself flexible, adaptive, and innovative."[44]

While Gardner does not use the teminology nor the theoretical position discussed here, an analysis of his writings readily suggests that his ordering of priorities in the matters of learning is intellect, morality, and technic. Using Gardner's concept of self-renewal, we may state that a self-renewing society is one that, by consciously assigning intellect first priority in formal learning, is enabled to take charge of its own social and cultural change processes. It is no longer driven by forces and processes that it does not understand; it is no longer blindly subject to those cyclical processes in which "any one society is apt to follow a roughly cyclical path through revolution, conservatism, and reaction, over and over again."[45]

What is being suggested by the writers whose works have been referred to above is this: because mind has entered the evolutionary process, it is possible for human beings to determine the nature and the bounds of their own social and cultural order. The term "self-renewing" has been suggested to describe the value orientation of such a society. Just as there is associated with each of the tripartite value orientations in Wallace's theory—that is, revolutionary, conservative, and reactionary—a philosophy of schooling that characteristically assigns priorities to the matters of learning in schools, so there is associated with the value orientation of the self-renewing society a particular philosophy of schooling that assigns priorities to the matters of learning. Thus we may add to Wallace's three societal types a fourth type, as shown in Figure 3.

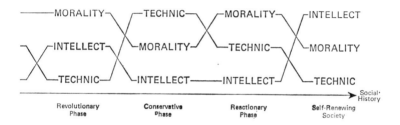

3. Educational Priorities in a Self-Renewing Society

This new ordering of priorities represents the conditions upon which a society can take command of its own future through continuous self-renewal. This is precisely what Makiguchi was proposing in his value-creating pedagogy. Makiguchi's work is not unique, however, simply because he proposed this approach to formal education and social reform. As suggested in chapter three, his proposals are not greatly different from those of Dewey or from those of a number of today's educators who are making similar proposals. Makiguchi's primary claim to uniqueness lies in the fact that Ikeda and Soka Gakkai are now attempting to implement his proposals, as Murata puts it, "on a grand scale."[46] Thus while the ideas of Dewey, for example, have greatly influenced and challenged untold numbers of people throughout the world and led to significant change upon the part of individual teachers and educators and in subsystems within a society, no attempt at implementing proposals involving this new ordering of priorities in the matters of learning has been made by a movement or organization, with the exception of Soka Gakkai, possessing potential to influence and change an entire society.

Certainly it is too early for any claim to be made that Soka Gakkai has been successful in this effort. Some informed observers wonder, for instance, if in the long run the rank-and-file members of the organization will support Ikeda in his elevation of intellect to first priority. It is not clear, either, how or to what extent the organization has been able to reconcile the relativistic and open stance toward which Ikeda is pointing with the absolutistic views and orientation of Nichiren Shoshu Buddhism. Another question many observers ask is whether Soka Gakkai, if it does gain increased power in Japanese society, will be able to remain true to its professed belief that power can be employed in the interests of the total society rather than in the interests of specific classes or groups. It should be recognized that some people are convinced that Soka Gakkai cannot be trusted with power. Carl Gross calls attention to arguments of some Japanese critics who contend that Ikeda, as the president of Soka Gakkai, is the highest authority in the organization and that he controls the decision-making in both Soka Gakkai and Komeito.[47] Such power is dangerous according to these critics. Even more critical of Soka Gakkai on this point is Hirotatsu Fujiwara, who declares in a recent book that Soka Gakkai is a serious threat to democracy in Japan.[48] These questions about Soka Gakkai cannot be answered at the present time. Yet if Soka Gakkai does succeed, even partially, in achieving its professed objectives, the result may well be one of the significant educational and sociological phenomena of the twentieth century. International educators should be aware of the pos-

sibilities as well as the dangers in the kind of social engineering
to which Soka Gakkai is committed.

<hr>

Makiguchi's Influence on Education

<hr>

Three general observations concerning Makiguchi's influence
on education and educators are suggested by the data here.
It is clear, first of all, that Makiguchi had very little influence
on Japanese education during his lifetime. As was noted in
chapter four, his educational ideas were largely rejected by his
contemporaries. Makiguchi was a man ahead of his time. The
general climate of Japanese society during the period in which
he lived was not right for the kind of educational and societal
reforms that he advocated. Neither on a theoretical nor on a
practical level can it be claimed that Makiguchi's educational
ideas have taken over Japanese education. The fact is that few
teachers in Japan, even today, know who Makiguchi was or
what he stood for. However, Makiguchi did influence Japanese
education indirectly in that both Toda and Ikeda picked up
and rewrote his major ideas and incorporated them into the
thought and practice of the Soka Gakkai organization. It
can also be said that Makiguchi did influence Japanese education in that Soka Gakkai is today attempting to implement his
ideas by establishing formal educational institutions based on
those ideas. In addition, Makiguchi's influence can be seen in
Komeito's concern with educational issues and problems.

Evidence of Komeito's interest in and involvement with educational matters is suggested by its one-hundred-year grand
plan for education. On the basis of interviews with Komeito
leaders in 1969 Gross concluded that the one-hundred-year

grand plan involves two major aims. These two aims are: "(1) to have each individual establish a philosophy of life, and (2) to elevate the standard of living, thereby improving society. In order to achieve this, educational goals will have to create values and promote the personality of each individual to the highest level. To implement this, Komeito has suggested the establishment of an Educational Planning Headquarters. This institution would have the responsibility for establishing long-range educational plans and policies. It would also have the responsibility for designing means to achieve these goals. This would be achieved by conferences of people from many fields who are directly or indirectly involved in the formal educational process. This conference would be divided into small committees to study the respective problems of education. Study would not only be theoretical, but would include actual proposals for the improvement of education. The final result would be a set of policies and plans for education with means of putting them into effect. In order to avoid dictatorship, the decisions would be those of the group. A further safeguard is suggested in a National Education Study Center, which would test the plans of the Educational Planning Headquarters."[49]

A second general observation is that what little direct influence Makiguchi has had on education has been limited to Japan. A few non-Japanese have begun to pick up and expose his ideas to the scrutiny of research, but those ideas have as yet had little influence on the educational thought and practice of other countries. This raises an interesting question. If Makiguchi's educational ideas were as advanced for his day and of the character suggested here, why was he not recognized by the educators of other countries? Makiguchi was saying and expressing in his writing many of the same criticisms and ideas about education that John Dewey was expressing at roughly the same period. Yet Makiguchi remained unknown, whereas

Dewey was recognized as a great educator and honored in many countries of the world.

Two factors may be cited for this neglect of Makiguchi by world educators. One is the simple fact that he was an Oriental. Educators have traditionally looked to Western sources for new ideas and insights. Until very recently the assumption of the superiority of Western culture was unquestioned, even in non-Western cultures. Thus in Makiguchi's day the idea that a Japanese could contribute significant educational and philosophical insights to international education would have been quite unacceptable, not only to Westerners but to most Japanese. A second factor in the neglect of Makiguchi by international educators is that of language. Even if non-Japanese educators had been predisposed to listen to Makiguchi, they would have been faced with the practical difficulty of their inability to communicate with him because of the language barrier. Since Makiguchi's writings were not available in translation and since Makiguchi himself never mastered English, non-Japanese educators did not have access to him or to his ideas.

A third observation that may be made about Makiguchi's influence on education is that although many of his ideas were novel for his day, some of those ideas are being recognized today as important aspects of effective educational practice. Educational practice in the average school, whether Japanese or non-Japanese, has changed little since Makiguchi's day. Evidence that this is the case in Japan is provided by a study that appeared in the *Asahi Shimbun* on June 4, 1971. This study indicates that not more than half of all elementary and junior high school students understand what teachers are attempting to teach them. Modern teachers and educators are becoming increasingly aware, however, of the soundness and merit of the kinds of educational ideas that Makiguchi advocated. Reference can be made, for example, to his opposition to memorization, his emphasis on the development of the creative potential of every student, his half-day school proposal with its implications not only for economy but for the involvement of community people in the educational process, and his concept of community study as the basis of curriculum. These ideas, which were central in Makiguchi's educational thought, are now coming to be central in current thinking about and projections of education of the future. In the study of the works of such prophetic educators as Makiguchi, the contemporary educator can gain valuable insights and understandings that will assist him in his efforts to provide effective educational experience for children and young people who are and will be participants in a postindustrial, global community.

Notes ————————————————————————————

1. William E. Drake, *Intellectual Foundations of Modern Education* (Columbus, Ohio: Charles E. Merrill Books, Inc., 1967), p. 275.

2. John L. Childs, *Education and the Philosophy of Experimentalism* (New York: The Century Company, 1931), p. 4.

3. Anthony F. C. Wallace, "Revitalization Movements," *American Anthropologist*, Vol. 58, No. 2, 1956, p. 265.

4. Anthony F. C. Wallace, "Schools in Revolutionary and Conservative Societies," in *Anthropology and Education*, ed. Frederick C. Gruber (Philadelphia: University of Pennsylvania Press, 1961), pp. 38–39.

5. Ibid., p. 40.
6. Ibid.

1   FAMILY LIFE AND ENVIRONMENTAL INFLUENCES

1. Satoshi Ikeda, *Makiguchi Tsunesaburo* (Tokyo: Nihon Sonoshobo, 1969), p. 23.
2. Ibid.
3. Robert Epp, "Japan's Century of Change: Intellectual Aspects," *Japan Christian Quarterly*, XXXV, No. 2 (Spring, 1969), pp. 72–74.
4. Ibid., p. 74.

2   PROFESSIONAL LIFE

1. S. Ikeda, *Makiguchi Tsunesaburo*, pp. 38–39.
2. Ibid., p. 43.
3. Ibid., pp. 41–42.
4. Ibid., pp. 31–33.
5. Ibid., pp. 44–45.
6. Ibid., p. 45.
7. Suketoshi Tanabe, Preface to *Soka Kyoikugaku Taikei* [The System of Value-Creating Pedagogy], by Tsunesaburo Makiguchi, reprinted in Tsunesaburo Makiguchi, *The Philosophy of Value*, ed. Josei Toda (Tokyo: Seikyo Press, 1964), p. 183.
8. Ibid. See also, Yoshihei Kodaira, *Soka Gakkai* (Tokyo: Otori Shoin 1962), p. 65.
9. Kiyoaki Murata, *Japan's New Buddhism* (New York & Tokyo: Walker/ Weatherhill, 1969), p. 73.
10. S. Ikeda, *Makiguchi Tsunesaburo*, pp. 27–28, 34.
11. Tsunesaburo Makiguchi, *Zenshu* [Complete Works], 5 vols. (Tokyo: Tozai Tetsugaku Shoin, 1965), 1:5.
12. S. Ikeda, *Makiguchi Tsunesaburo*, p. 42.
13. Victor Kobayashi, *John Dewey in Japanese Educational Thought* (Ann Arbor: University of Michigan School of Education, 1964), pp. 37–38.

3   VALUE-CREATING PEDAGOGY

1. Makiguchi, *Zenshu*, 1:4.
2. Kobayashi, *John Dewey*, p. 154.
3. S. Ikeda, *Makiguchi Tsunesaburo*, p. 91.
4. Makiguchi, *Zenshu*, 1:6.
5. Tsunesaburo Makiguchi, *The Philosophy of Value*, ed. Josei Toda (Tokyo: Seikyo Press, 1964), p. 4.

6. Noah S. Brannen, "Soka Gakkai's Theory of Value," *Contemporary Religions in Japan*, V, No. 2 (June, 1964), p. 143.

7. Lester Ward, *Glimpses of the Cosmos*, 6 vols. (New York: G. P. Putnam's Sons, 1913), 4:155.

8. Makiguchi, *Philosophy of Value*, pp. 9, 22.

9. Ibid., pp. 92–93.

10. Ibid., p. 83.

11. Ibid., p. 84.

12. Ibid., pp. 15–16.

13. Makiguchi, *Zenshu*, 1:60.

14. Makiguchi, *Philosophy of Value*, p. 17.

15. Brannen, "Soka Gakkai's Theory of Value," pp. 146–47.

16. Michael Novak, *The Experience of Nothingness* (New York: Harper & Row, 1970), p. 105.

17. Theodore Brameld, *The Climactic Decades* (New York: Prager, 1970), p. 125.

18. David J. Bond, "The Fact-Value Myth," *Social Education*, XXXIV, No. 2 (February, 1970), p. 190.

19. Makiguchi, *Philosophy of Value*, p. 20.

20. Ibid., pp. 20–21.

21. Makiguchi, *Zenshu*, 1:131.

22. Ibid., p. 125.

23. Ibid., p. 129.

24. Ibid., p. 15.

25. Ibid., 2:313.

26. Ibid., 1:18.

27. Ibid., pp. 33–35.

28. Ibid., p. 33.

29. Ibid., pp. 33–34.

30. Ibid., p. 34.

31. Ibid., p. 11.

32. Ibid., 5:52.

33. Ibid., 2:293.

34. Ibid., p. 253.

35. Ibid., pp. 290–91.

36. Ibid., 5:460.

37. Kobayashi, *John Dewey*, p. 24.

38. Judith Groch, *The Right to Create* (Boston: Little, Brown and Company, 1969), p. 182.

39. Yasumasa Oshima, "Education in Japan 1945–1963," *Journal of Social and Political Ideas in Japan*, Vol. 1, No. 3 (December, 1963), pp. 5–6.

40. Ronald S. Anderson, "Japan: Three Epochs of Modern Education," U. S. Department of Health, Education, and Welfare, *Bulletin*, 1959, No. 11, pp. 205–8.

41. Ibid., pp. 31–32.
42. Murata, *Japan's New Buddhism*, p. 87.
43. Kobayashi, *John Dewey*, p. 27.
44. Van Cleve Morris, review of *Crisis in the Classroom: The Remaking of American Education* by Charles Silberman, *Educational Studies*, II, Nos. 1 and 2 (Spring–Summer, 1971), pp. 46–47.

4 MAKIGUCHI AND THE SOKA GAKKAI MOVEMENT

1. Murata, *Japan's New Buddhism*, p. 76.
2. Makiguchi, *Zenshu*, 3:160 and 4: 577.
3. Murata, *Japan's New Buddhism*, p. 76.
4. Tsunesaburo Makiguchi, *Soka Kyoikugaku Taikei* [The System of Value-Creating Pedagogy] (Tokyo: Fuzanbo, 1930), Vol. 1, pp. 87–89.
5. Makiguchi, *Philosophy of Value*, p. 159.
6. Brannen, "Soka Gakkai's Theory of Value," pp. 151–52.
7. Makiguchi, *Philosophy of Value*, p. 125.
8. *The Nichiren Shoshu Sokagakkai* (Tokyo: Seikyo Press, 1966), pp. 46–47.
9. Murata, *Japan's New Buddhism*, pp. 88–90.
10. Ibid., p. 89.
11. Ibid., p. 90.
12. S. Ikeda, *Makiguchi Tsunesaburo*, p. 185.
13. Murata, *Japan's New Buddhism*, pp. 93–94.
14. Quoted in Murata, *Japan's New Buddhism*, p. 94.
15. Quoted in Murata, *Japan's New Buddhism*, p. 94.
16. Murata, *Japan's New Buddhism*, pp. 95–98.
17. Ibid., p. 16.
18. Ibid., p. 102.
19. Quoted in Murata, *Japan's New Buddhism*, p. 104.
20. H. Neill McFarland, *The Rush Hour of the Gods* (New York: The Macmillan Company, 1967), p. 4.
21. Quoted in Murata, *Japan's New Buddhism*, p. 104.
22. Quoted in Murata, *Japan's New Buddhism*, p. 104.
23. Kazuo Kasahara, "Soka Gakkai and Komeito: The Advance of a New Religion into Politics," *Japan Quarterly*, Vol. XIV, No. 3 (July–September, 1967), p. 313.
24. Ibid., p. 314.
25. James Allen Dator, *Sōka Gakkai, Builders of the Third Civilization* (Seattle: University of Washington Press, 1969), p. 139.
26. Noah S. Brannen, *Sōka Gakkai: Japan's Militant Buddhists* (Richmond, Va.: John Knox Press, 1968), p. 15.
27. Ibid., p. 102.
28. Ibid., p. 103.
29. Fujio Ikado, "Trend and Problems of New Religions in Urban So-

ciety," in Kiyomi Morioka and William H. Newell, *The Sociology of Japanese Religion* (Leiden: E. J. Brill, 1968), p. 104.

30. Skelton T. Lane, "Social Movements and Social Change: The Soka Gakkai of Japan" (Ph.D. diss., University of California, Berkeley, 1968), p. 87.

31. Daisaku Ikeda, "Great Cultural Movement: From Mechanistic to Humanistic Society" (Presidential address to 33rd General Meeting of Soka Gakkai, May 3, 1970), *Seikyo Times*, June, 1970.

32. Murata, *Japan's New Buddhism*, p. 125.

33. McFarland, *Rush Hour of the Gods.* p. 232.

34. Daisaku Ikeda, *Complete Works of Daisaku Ikeda* (Tokyo: Seikyo Press, 1968), Vol. 1, pp. 98, 108–10.

35. Ibid., p. 6.

36. Ibid., pp. 113–14.

37. Ibid., p. 5.

38. Ibid., p. 7.

39. Ibid., pp. 109–10.

40. Ibid., p. 12.

41. Ibid., p. 83.

42. Ibid., p. 98.

43. Ibid., p. 83.

44. Murata, *Japan's New Buddhism*, p. 125.

45. S. Ikeda, *Makiguchi Tsunesaburo*, p. 206.

46. *Newsweek*, January 19, 1970, p. 46.

47. D. Ikeda, *Complete Works*, p. 11.

48. Ibid., p. 131.

49. Ibid., p. 84.

50. Ibid., p. 89.

51. Daisaku Ikeda, "Youth Let's Advance Toward a New Day" (Presidential address to 31st General Meeting of Soka Gakkai, May 3, 1968), pp. 6–8.

52. Murata, *Japan's New Buddhism*, p. 76.

5 EDUCATION IN A SELF-RENEWING SOCIETY

1. Seymour M. Lipset, *Revolution and Counterrevolution* (New York: Basic Books, 1968), p. 6.

2. Ibid.

3. Wallace, "Schools in Revolutionary and Conservative Societies,' p. 29.

4. Ibid.

5. Ibid.

6. Ibid., pp. 29–30.

7. Ibid., p. 31.

8. Ibid., pp. 31–32.
9. Ibid., p. 37.
10. Frederick C. Gruber, ed., *Anthropology and Education* (Philadelphia: University of Pennsylvania Press, 1961), p. 37.
11. Wallace, "Schools in Revolutionary and Conservative Societies," pp. 38–39.
12. Ibid., p. 40.
13. Ibid.
14. Ibid.
15. Wallace, "Revitalization Movements," p. 265.
16. Wallace, "Schools in Revolutionary and Conservative Societies," p. 41
17. Ibid., pp. 41–42.
18. Ibid., p. 43.
19. Ibid., p. 44.
20. Ibid.
21. Ibid., p. 45.
22. Ibid.
23. C. Wright Mills, *The Power Elite* (New York: Oxford University Press, 1956), p. 317.
24. Wallace, "Schools in Revolutionary and Conservative Societies," p. 47.
25. Ibid., pp. 47–48.
26. Ibid., pp. 48–49.
27. Gruber, *Anthropology and Education*, p. 49.
28. Wallace, "Revitalization Movements," p. 277.
29. Wallace, "Schools in Revolutionary and Conservative Societies," p. 43.
30. John Gardner, *Self-Renewal* (New York: Harper & Row, 1963), pp. 40–42.
31. Arthur Koestler, *The God That Failed* (New York: Bantam Books, 1952), p. 13.
32. Lester Ward, *Applied Sociology* (New York: Ginn and Company, 1906), pp. 280–81, 337–38. See also Ward's address, "Education and Progress," delivered at Ruskin College in England in 1909, in his *Glimpses of the Cosmos*, 6:337–40. It will be more accessible to most readers in *Lester Ward and the Welfare State*, ed. Henry S. Commager (New York: Bobbs-Merrill Company, 1967), pp. 409–15.
33. Wallace, "Schools in Revolutionary and Conservative Societies," p. 52.
34. Ibid., pp. 53–54.
35. Arthur Koestler, *Darkness at Noon* (New York: The New American Library, 1961), p. 144.

36. Suzanne Keller, *Beyond the Ruling Class* (New York: Random House, 1963), p. 264.

37. C. Wright Mills, *The Sociological Imagination* (New York: Oxford University Press, 1959), pp. 4–5.

38. Ibid., pp. 10–11.

39. Eleanor Roosevelt, *Tomorrow Is Now* (New York: Harper & Row, 1963), p. 66.

40. Drake, *Intellectual Foundations of Modern Education*, p. 235.

41. Ibid., pp. 343–45.

42. Gardner, *Self-Renewal*, pp. 21–22.

43. Ibid., pp. 22–23.

44. Ibid., p. 26.

45. Wallace, "Schools in Revolutionary and Conservative Societies," p. 40.

46. Murata, *Japan's New Buddhism*, p. 76.

47. Carl H. Gross, *Sokagakkai and Education* (East Lansing: Michigan State University, Institute for International Studies, 1970), pp. 72–73.

48. Hirotatsu Fujiwara, *I Denounce Soka Gakkai* (Tokyo: Nisshin Hodo, 1970), pp. 78–87, 244–46.

49. Gross, *Sokagakkai and Education*, pp. 48–49. See also Special Committee for University and High School Affairs, *Draft for Komeito Educational Policy*, No. 2, April, 1970.

Bibliography

PRIMARY SOURCES: BOOKS

Ikeda, Daisaku. *Complete Works of Daisaku Ikeda.* (Originally published as *Ikeda Kaicho Zenshu.* Tokyo, Seikyo Press, 1967.) Vol. 1. Tokyo, Seikyo Press, 1968.

———. *Shido Memo* [Guidance Memo]. Tokyo, Seikyo Press, 1966.

Makiguchi, Tsunesaburo. *Jinsei Chirigaku* [The Geography of Human Life]. Tokyo, Fuzanbo, 1903.

———. *The Philosophy of Value.* (Originally published as *Kachiron.* Ed. and supplemented by Josei Toda. Tokyo, Sokagakkai, 1953.) Tokyo, Seikyo Press, 1964.

163

————. *Soka Kyoikugaku Taikei* [The System of Value-Creating Peda-
gogy]. Vol. 1. Tokyo, Fuzanbo, 1930.
————. *Zenshu* [Complete Works]. 5 vols. Tokyo, Tozai Tetsugaku
Shoin, 1965.
The Nichiren Shoshu Sokagakkai. Tokyo, Seikyo Press, 1966.
Toda, Josei. *Lecture on the Sutra: Hoben and Juryo Chapters.* (Originally
published as *Hoben-pon Juryo-hon Kogi.* Tokyo, Seikyo Press, 1968.)
Tokyo, Seikyo Press, 1968.

PRIMARY SOURCES: ARTICLES, PAMPHLETS, AND PERIODICALS

Ikeda, Daisaku. "Great Cultural Movement: From Mechanistic to
Humanistic Society." Presidential address to the 33rd General Meet-
ing of Soka Gakkai, May 3, 1970. *Seikyo Times,* June, 1970.
————. "Youth Let's Advance Toward a New Day." Presidential
address to 31st General Meeting of Soka Gakkai, May 3, 1968. Tokyo,
Seikyo Press, 1968.
Kachi Sozo [The Creation of Value]. Tokyo, Soka Kyoiku Gakkai, 1941
Kankyo [Environment]. Tokyo, Jobundo, 1930.
Komeito. *Eighth National Convention Program.* Tokyo, The Komeito Party
Publishing Office, June, 1970.
Makiguchi, Tsunesaburo. *Soka Kyoikuho no Kagakuteki Choshukyoteki Jikken
Shomei* [Practical Experimentation in Value-Creating Educational
Methods Through Science and Supreme Religion]. Tokyo, Soka
Kyoiku Gakkai, 1937.
Soka University. Tokyo, The Soka University Preparatory Foundation, Soka-
gakkai, nd.
Special Committee for University and High School Affairs. *Draft for
Komeito Educational Policy.* No. 2. Tokyo, Komeito, April, 1970.
Taizen Seikatsu Jisshoroku [Witness to Abundant Life]. Nos. 4 and 5. Tokyo,
Soka Kyoiku Gakkai, 1942.
Todai. Tokyo, Todai Kanko Kai, March, 1971.

PRIMARY SOURCES: UNPUBLISHED MATERIALS

Makiguchi, Tsunesaburo. Post-card messages written from prison to
daughter-in-law, Sadako.
Nakabayashi, Kozaburo. Unpublished manuscript.

SECONDARY SOURCES: BOOKS

Anesaki, Masaharu. *Nichiren, the Buddhist Prophet.* Cambridge, Harvard
University Press, 1949.
Brameld, Theodore. *The Climactic Decades.* New York, Prager, 1970.

Brannen, Noah S. *Sōka Gakkai: Japan's Militant Buddhists.* Richmond, Virginia, John Knox Press, 1968.

Brown, George I. *Human Teaching for Human Learning: An Introduction to Confluent Education.* New York, Viking Press, 1971.

Childs, John L. *Education and the Philosophy of Experimentalism.* New York, The Century Company, 1931.

Commager, Henry Steele, ed. *Lester Ward and the Welfare State.* New York Bobbs-Merrill Company, 1967.

Dator, James Allen. *Sōka Gakkai, Builders of the Third Civilization.* Seattle, University of Washington Press, 1969.

Drake, William E. *Intellectual Foundations of Modern Education.* Columbus, Ohio, Charles E. Merrill Books, Inc., 1967.

Fujiwara, Hirotatsu. *I Denounce Soka Gakkai.* (Originally published as *Sōka Gakkai o Kiru.* Tokyo, Nisshin Hodo, 1969.) Tokyo, Nisshin Hodo, 1970.

Gardner, John. *Self-Renewal.* New York, Harper & Row, 1963.

Groch, Judith. *The Right to Create.* Boston, Little, Brown and Company, 1969.

Gross, Carl H. *Sokagakkai and Education.* East Lansing, Michigan State University, Institute for International Studies, 1970.

Harrington, Michael. *Accidental Century.* New York, The Macmillan Company, 1965.

Idditti, Shimosa. *The Life of Marquis Shigenobu Okuma: A Maker of New Japan.* Tokyo, Hokuseido Press, 1941.

Ike, Nobutaka. *The Beginnings of Political Democracy in Japan.* Baltimore, Johns Hopkins University Press, 1950.

Ikeda, Satoshi. *Makiguchi Tsunesaburo.* Tokyo, Nihon Sonoshobo, 1969.

Keller, Suzanne. *Beyond the Ruling Class.* New York, Random House, 1963.

Kobayashi, Victor. *John Dewey in Japanese Educational Thought.* Ann Arbor, University of Michigan School of Education, 1964.

Kodaira, Yoshihei. *Sōka Gakkai.* Tokyo, Otari Shoin, 1962.

Koestler, Arthur. *Darkness at Noon.* New York, The New American Library, 1961.

————. *The God That Failed.* New York, Bantam Books, 1952.

Lane, Skelton T. "Social Movements and Social Change: The Soka Gakkai of Japan." Ph.D. dissertation, University of California, Berkeley, 1968.

Lipset, Seymour M. *Revolution and Counterrevolution.* New York, Basic Books, 1968.

McFarland, H. Neill. *The Rush Hour of the Gods.* New York, The Macmillan Company, 1967.

Mills, C. Wright. *The Power Elite.* New York, Oxford University Press, 1956.

————. *The Sociological Imagination.* New York, Oxford University Press, 1959.

———. *Sociology and Pragmatism: The Higher Learning in America.* New York, Paine-Whitman Publishers, 1964.

Murata, Kiyoaki. *Japan's New Buddhism.* New York and Tokyo, Walker/Weatherhill, 1969.

Novak, Michael. *The Experience of Nothingness.* New York, Harper & Row, 1970.

Passin, Herbert. *Society and Education in Japan.* New York, Columbia University, Teachers College, Bureau of Publications, 1965.

Piovesana, Gino K. *Recent Japanese Philosophical Thought, 1862–1962.* Tokyo, Enderle Bookstore, 1963.

Reischauer, Edwin O.; Fairbank, John K.; and Craig, Albert M. *East Asia: The Modern Transformation.* Boston, Houghton Mifflin, 1965.

Roosevelt, Eleanor. *Tomorrow Is Now.* New York, Harper & Row, 1963.

Silberman, Charles. *Crisis in the Classroom: The Remaking of American Education.* New York, Random House, 1970.

Smith, Thomas C. *Political Change and Industrial Development in Japan: Government Enterprise, 1868–1880.* Stanford, California, Stanford University Press, 1955.

Ward, Lester. *Applied Sociology.* New York, Ginn and Company, 1906.

———. *Glimpses of the Cosmos.* 6 vols. New York, G. P. Putnam's Sons, 1913.

White, James W. *The Sokagakkai and Mass Society.* Stanford, California, Stanford University Press, 1970.

SECONDARY SOURCES: ARTICLES, PAMPHLETS, AND PERIODICALS

Anderson, Ronald S. "Japan: Three Epochs of Modern Education." U. S. Department of Health, Education, and Welfare, *Bulletin,* 1959, No. 11.

Bond, David J. "The Fact-Value Myth." *Social Education* XXXIV, No. 2 (February, 1970): 190.

Brannen, Noah S. "Soka Gakkai's Theory of Value." *Contemporary Religions in Japan* Vol. V, No. 2 (June, 1964): 143.

Epp, Robert. "Japan's Century of Change: Intellectual Aspects." *Japan Christian Quarterly* XXXV, No. 2 (Spring, 1969): 72–74.

Ikado, Fujio. "Trend and Problems of New Religions in Urban Society." In Kiyomi Morioka and William H. Newell, *The Sociology of Japanese Religion,* pp. 101–17. Leiden, E. J. Brill, 1968.

Kasahara, Kazuo. "Soka Gakkai and Komeito: The Advance of a New Religion into Politics." *Japan Quarterly* XIV, No. 3 (July–September, 1967): 313.

Morris, Van Cleve. Review of *Crisis in the Classroom: The Remaking of American Education* by Charles Silberman. *Educational Studies* II, Nos. 1 and 2 (Spring–Summer, 1971): 46–47.

Newsweek. January 19, 1970, p. 46.

Oshima, Yasumasa. "Education in Japan 1945–1963." *Journal of Social and Political Ideas in Japan* Vol. 1, No. 3 (December, 1963): 5–6.

Wallace, Anthony F. C. "Revitalization Movements." *American Anthropologist* Vol. 58, No. 2 (1956): 264–81.

————. "Schools in Revolutionary and Conservative Societies." In *Anthropology and Education*, ed. by Frederick C. Gruber, pp. 25–54. Philadelphia, University of Pennsylvania Press, 1961.

Index

Anderson, Ronald S., 82
ankoku (securing the peace of the land), 111-12
Arahama-mura, 25, 26. 37

Bond, David J., 55
Brameld, Theodore, 55
Brannen, Noah S., 50, 53, 92-93, 107, 108
Brown, George I., 54-55

bunka kyoiku, see cultural education

Childs, John L., 21
Clean Government Party, *see* Komeito
community study, 36, 39-40, 86, 154
  application of, in education, 64, 74-77
  function of, in education, 60-62

169

Kasahara, Kazuo, 105–6
Keller, Suzanne, 145
Kobayashi, Victor, 44–45, 48, 79–80
Koestler, Arthur, 142, 144–45
Komeito (Clean Government Party), 22, 116–17, 150
and education, 151–52
kosen rufu (spreading Buddhism through the world), 102, 104
kyodoka, see community study
Kyodoka Kenkyu (Research Studies in Folk Culture), 39

Lane, Skelton T., 110
learning, 18, 60, 135–36; *see also* matters of learning
circumstances of, 127, 129–30
divisions of, 127–29, 130
Lotus Sutra, 100, 101, 102, 103, 119

Makiguchi, Kuma (wife), 27, 34–35
Makiguchi, Kumataro (father-in-law), 27
Makiguchi, Tsunesaburo (born Chohichi Watanabe); *see also* Makiguchi's philosophy of value; value-creating pedagogy
arrest and imprisonment, 27–28, 29, 81, 98–99, 100
children, 27–28, 34–35, 37
and community study, 36, 39–40, 60–62, 64, 74, 76–77, 86, 154
compared with Dewey, 19–20, 21, 85–87, 152–53
conversion to Nichiren Shoshu, 42, 91–92, 93, 138
criticism of Japanese education, 29, 32, 47–49, 57–59, 63–64, 75–76, 77, 95, 137
death, 28, 98
Dewey's influence on, 44, 45, 83, 85
early life, 25–27

educational thought, 43, 47–49, 51, 56–64, 74–78, 83–84, 95, 121
as founder of Soka Gakkai, 21, 93–94, 122–23
half-day school proposal, 76–78, 154
influence on education, 95–97, 151–54
Nichiren Shoshu's influence on, 41–43, 91–93, 96, 103–4, 138
rejection of, in Japan, 19, 21, 59–60, 78, 89–90, 95–96, 151, 153
religious convictions, 91–93, 97
shift from educational to religious orientation, 42, 90–92 96–98, 138–39
and Soka Kyoiku Gakkai, 93–94, 97–98, 118
standing in academic world, 35, 59–60, 84, 85
as teacher and educator, 27, 31–32, 34, 38–41, 84
and Toda, 41, 84, 98, 99–100
views on geography and education, 32–33
Ward's influence on, 45, 83, 85, 143
as writer, 33, 34–38, 41–44, 64, 85, 92–93, 113
WORKS:
Jinsei Chirigaku (The Geography of Human Life), 36–37, 39–40, 42–43, 45, 92
Kyodoka Kenkyu (Research Studies in Folk Culture), 39
Philosophy of Value, The (Kachiron), 92–93
Soka Kyoikugaku Taikei (The System of Value-Creating Pedagogy), 38, 41–42, 43–45, 49, 60, 63, 92, 93, 94, 98
Soka Kyoikuho no Kagakuteki Choshukyoteki Jikken Shomei (Practi-